HEALED
A Memoir

LACOLE ROBINSON

authorHOUSE

AuthorHouse™
1663 Liberty Drive
Bloomington, IN 47403
www.authorhouse.com
Phone: 833-262-8899

© 2022 Lacole Robinson. All rights reserved.

No part of this book may be reproduced, stored in a retrieval system, or transmitted by any means without the written permission of the author.

Published by AuthorHouse 10/25/2022

ISBN: 978-1-6655-7451-8 (sc)
ISBN: 978-1-6655-7452-5 (hc)
ISBN: 978-1-6655-7453-2 (e)

Library of Congress Control Number: 2022919891

Print information available on the last page.

Any people depicted in stock imagery provided by Getty Images are models, and such images are being used for illustrative purposes only.
Certain stock imagery © Getty Images.

This book is printed on acid-free paper.

Because of the dynamic nature of the Internet, any web addresses or links contained in this book may have changed since publication and may no longer be valid. The views expressed in this work are solely those of the author and do not necessarily reflect the views of the publisher, and the publisher hereby disclaims any responsibility for them.

New International Version (NIV) Holy Bible, New International Version®, NIV® Copyright ©1973, 1978, 1984, 2011 by Biblica, Inc.® Used by permission. All rights reserved worldwide.

Contents

Acknowledgments vii
Around 1997 & 1998 1
Around 1990 14
Around 1999 18
Around 2000 43
Around October 2001 47
Around June 2001 55
Around 2002 61
Around February 2002 68
Around 2003 & 2004 70
Around 2005 75
Around 2006 82
Around December 19, 2006 87
Around January 24, 2007 89
Around 2008 103
Around 2009 106
Around 2010 115
Around 2011 119
Around October 3, 2012 127
Around August 23, 2013 131
Around August 20, 2015 137
Around April 3, 2015 140
Around June 2015 143

Around March 20, 2017 148
Around October 17, 2017 151
Around January 2018.. 157
Around February 2018 159
Around May 22, 2018.. 164
Around June 16, 2018.. 165
Around August 8, 2019 172
Around September 2019 174
Around November 28, 2019 176

Acknowledgments

I want to first and foremost thank my heavenly father from above for getting me through all the struggles, trails, and tribulations giving me something to write about. For giving me the strength emotionally during this process it was emotionally draining reliving the past, but therapeutic at the same time. Now I'm healed. I wanna give a special shoutout to my husband for inspiring me to write a book. My sisters for the love and support that was giving. I also want to take the time to thank my editor Teynia Lee from New York and my amazing graphic designer Xavier Comas from Barcelona, Spain. For teaching me so much through this process, and for all the patience they endured with me being a first-time writer not knowing anything about becoming an author. It was tough many thanks too you all. I highly appreciate you! And I want to give myself a pat on the back for believing in myself and completing God's purpose with still more to come.

Around 1997 & 1998

Southeast San Diego 50th, Down the block from the infamous car wash owned by the local street hustlers and the aptly named Four Corners of Death located on Imperial and Euclid. Living there was the true definition of poverty and dysfunction.

Honestly, you do not know what you will wake up to when you live in this part of town, with gang members, crack heads, prostitutes, you name it.

Usually, I woke up every morning around 6:00 am to brush my teeth and wash my face. I would try to shower the night before, as I had to dress my two younger sisters, Lakeyna and Latrice, each morning too. I also had to do my doughnut bun, which took forever.

My bun was never popping. My hair was not that long and I would grab it so tight that it would hurt while trying to fit it in a ponytail. But it never went into a fan ponytail, which was popular back then. My homegirls Sa'adha and Aaliyah would rock the mess out of those fan ponytails. They had enough hair to do all the styles. It was what it was, and I worked with what I had. I did what I had to do to make myself look good, at least to my standards.

I thought I was cute, and that is all that mattered. Sometimes, I would get lucky and my cousin Dada would braid my hair in cornrows or style me a ponytail with extensions. Other than that, it was usually the donut bun, and it was not looking good.

I never bothered to wake my mom up in the morning. She was always in a deep coma on the couch, with the television on from the night before, covered by a sheet full of cigarette burns. She usually fell asleep with the cigarette in her hand from taking too many prescription drugs. Codeine and Soma were her favorites and most common choice.

It was a demanding situation. She never helped me get the girls ready for school. All she would do is be grouchy and yell at me for whatever reason, like everything was my fault, and that just made mornings worse. There were times I really wanted to cuss her out, but I knew she would tear me up and I wouldn't dare fight my mom because I had way too much respect for her. So, for whatever reason, I kept my thoughts to myself.

Instead, I did what I had to do for me and my sisters. Regardless of what my mom was going through, somebody had to do it, since they were too young to take care of themselves. I still thank God that we survived that drama.

I was curious about why my mom and dad didn't work out. I would ask my mom why she didn't love my dad the way he said he loved her. She stated that she was with my dad because she was lonely and because he had a job with a nice car and he was funny, but she never really loved him. She was lonely, and that was one of the reasons she would abuse her addiction and why she could never let go of the other things she suffered from as a child.

She was depressed and living in the past. She really needed a pastor or a counselor. I believe counseling could have helped her out of the cycle of poor decisions she made with men. She needed someone to help uplift her spirit and tell her she was important and beautiful, both inside and out. She needed support. But she never got it. She lived in depression, and it was incredibly sad to see her that way. I couldn't do anything to help her. Though I would always tell her how much I loved her, that was still never good enough.

I always thought my dad and my mom would have made it together if they would have gotten married, did what was right for me, and left the drugs alone. All my mom needed was a good man to love her and treat her right. My dad was capable of that. They were remarkably similar people. They were both good people.

Whenever I saw them together, they were always laughing and would always get along, so why weren't they together? I wondered. My dad says Mom was the only woman he ever loved, and I believed it. But I don't think she really gave him a chance. I honestly think she might have been one of the reasons my dad didn't want to do right, and why he stayed in his heavy addiction. He knew she did not love him the way he desired to be loved.

My dad was desperate for the type of love from a woman that he didn't receive from his own mother. How he was molested as a young boy by one of his older cousin's. He once told me that his mother didn't love him. He was looking for security and trust in a woman, and my mom could not give him either, because she did not know how to. And, well, that was not her fault. She claims all her dad would do was get drunk after work, come home, and beat her and her mother.

My dad's mother got remarried to her new baby's father when she moved to Los Angeles, leaving my dad all alone in San Diego with his father and whoever else. Which the situation with his father was strange to me, his father had got remarried to a lady name Sarah that couldn't stand the sight of my dad.

Anyway, dad said he was so excited when he found out my mom was pregnant and having a girl. He knew I would love him unconditionally, no matter what, and he was right. I really did love my dad with all my heart. You couldn't tell me nothing wrong about my father, drugs or not.

As a kid, I knew my dad was on drugs. One day, I rode with him to Wrigley's, which was a grocery store on Euclid and Federal. He was going to buy food for me and my sisters.

Outside the store, we saw one of my neighborhood uncles named Big Pee. He wasn't really my uncle, but I loved Uncle Pee. He was the man growing up. I was too young to really know what he was doing that day;

I just knew it wasn't right. Anyway, he saw me and my dad, and he asked my dad for money. My dad didn't have it, so Uncle Pee told me to step out of my dad's nice white Cadillac and then he threw a brick through the front windshield.

He knew my dad wasn't going to do anything because he didn't. Uncle Pee apologized to me and said he didn't want me to see this, but he had no choice. I started crying. I felt bad for my dad.

I remember going to visit my grandmother, my dad's mom, when I was about five years old. I went to Los Angeles to see her and her family, my auntie Pansy, and my uncle Lagina, and her husband, big Lagina. I had so much fun that I didn't want to go home. I remember my auntie doing my hair, dressing me pretty, and painting my nails. My grandmother didn't want to send me back either, but my mom insisted and got me back. My mom couldn't stand my grandmother, and that explains why she didn't like my dad. She would say his mom messed him up.

To this day, there is one thing I question about my visit to Los Angeles. I was too young to understand back then, but if I'm not mistaken, my grandmother lost her husband when I was there visiting. I remember being in the garage with him and him falling to the ground, and my grandmother rushing in, panicked, and then she called the paramedics. I didn't see him ever again after that or questioned the situation.

My mom would always say things like my dad was ugly and that he beat her. I never saw him beat her though. But what I did see was my mom hitting my dad over the head with a glass bottle once.

That time, the police took her to jail. I remember my dad telling me to wave bye to Mommy in the back of the police car, and I was saying "bye, Mommy." That's something I'll never forget.

She was home the next day and my dad didn't press charges. I was happy she made it back. I was happy to see her.

I loved it when my parents were together. Being the only kid around was fun from what I can remember growing up, and my mom didn't seem so sad when my dad was around, regardless of what she would say. Even so, it was clear that she was unhappy, and she hated every bit of it.

I remember my mom always telling me I was ugly when I was born. The doctor told her she was having a boy, and she did not want a girl. The whole time my mom was pregnant up until the last few months, she thought she was having a boy.

She hated the fact that I looked like my dad. She told me how she was mad when she found out she was pregnant, and how that made her hate him even more. The only reason she stayed pregnant, she said, was because she had recently lost her mom and she felt lonely, otherwise she would have gone to get another abortion.

Grandma Stella, my mom's mom, passed away from overdosing on prescription pills in her mid-forties. My mom had found her on the couch dead. She said she had peed on herself, and that is how she knew she had passed away.

One of her brothers was on the floor, crying. Mom was close to her mother and she would show me pictures of my grandmother all the time and tell me how she was a very pretty lady, and my mom looked just like her.

Mom took the death extremely hard, and shortly after that, she started doing the same drugs while pregnant with me. Nine months later, I was born into this messed up world, an ugly baby my mom didn't want to have.

Sometimes I wish I could have told her, I didn't ask to be here, and I would not have minded if she would have stuck me back up in her, reversed the entire process of having me. I did not sign up for this. This ain't the life I wanted to live. You had me; I didn't have you.

This morning, I remember fixing the hanger on the back of the television to get a better signal. Bill Clinton was on the news top headline. They were talking about impeaching him. I didn't know too much about politics back then, but what I did know was that I liked him as our president. What I liked about him I didn't know, honestly. It was that he played the saxophone and smoked marijuana. I thought marijuana was okay because all my uncles smoked.

I should have paid more attention in social studies class. School was always boring, and I was always distracted thinking about other things, like what I'm going to feed my sisters when we get home, what my mom was doing, and whether she was okay or not. These were things I should not have been worrying about as a child. And having to worry about them was one of the reasons why I never wanted to further my education. I was just too distracted. It got to the point that I had to be in Special Ed classes because my grades had dropped to D's and F's. I had a short attention span. I could never stay focused or remember anything the teacher was saying.

I would get clowned so bad at school for being in those classes. Especially by my play brother Reg. I would hate to see him coming. It was very humiliating, but by being in those classes made me a C average student and that's what helped me graduate. Being in high school and trying to take care of my little sisters was difficult at times. I had too many responsibilities. But one thing that really stuck with me was my mom always saying, all she knows is, I better walk across that stage and get a diploma.

As I leave the bathroom from doing my hair, I go to wake up my sisters from the room we share.

Tapping them on the booties, I say, "Lakeyna, Trice, get up, we got to go."

Keyna was always the harder one to wake up. She was the middle child and exceedingly difficult to deal with. She was a chocolate baby with thick girly hair — and she was adorable! I remember when Lakeyna was born on March 21st, 1992. I was so thrilled. I would treat her like my own real baby.

I didn't know why, but when she got old enough to talk, she started telling on me every chance she got. I would want to whoop her. I was the only one sacrificing for your little butt and you want to tell on me? I couldn't believe it.

Not many of my friends knew about how my family lived. One day, my homeboys Rana and David came over to use our phone because one of them needed to call his sister. She lived near me and she wasn't answering the door. He started clowning me that my phone didn't match the receiver. The top part of the phone was black, and the bottom part was clear with all these colors. It was pieced together from two different phones, and it did not hang up all the way either. It was so embarrassing that I wanted to fall apart or disappear. I knew what was coming when they asked to use the phone, but it would have been more embarrassing to say I didn't have a phone. I never heard the last of it.

My mom wasn't home that day, thank God. She would have been on the couch, high as a kite like always making the situation worse. That would have been even more embarrassing to explain to my homeboys.

As soon as my mom got back, Lakeyna made sure she told on me, that I had boys in the house. I for sure got slapped around for that, and it was terrible having to choose between getting clowned or slapped.

I couldn't win for losing.

Latrice was the total opposite. She would often lie for me, saying no, I didn't do it. She was the cutest baby. She didn't say much as a kid or cry. She was very soft-spoken and quiet.

Her hair was a different texture from Keyna's, a lot finer, and she had a lighter complexion compared to Keyna, too. But otherwise, they looked just alike. People would ask if they were twins, but they were a year apart and had different dads.

Keyna and Trice, still sleepy, would say in their whiny voices, "Coley." They nicknamed me Coley because they couldn't pronounce Lacole. I loved it. I thought it was the cutest thing ever.

They never wanted to wake up. And sometimes when they did wake up, they would be hungry, from going to sleep with barely anything in their stomachs the night before.

With a little more pushing and prodding, they would get up and put their clothes on. I often fed them cereal if there was any Cheerios or Kix in the house. Those were the two cereals my mom got from W.I.C.

W.I.C, which stands for Women, Infants, and Children, gave welfare assistance to low-income parents with children under the age of eight. Unfortunately, my father, James, was away in prison at the time serving a ten-year sentence, his second strike for robbery and drug abuse, so he was no help.

After my sisters ate their cereal, if there was any, I would do their hair, then off to school we went. They went to Kennedy Elementary, conveniently across the street from Lincoln High School, where I went, otherwise I would have been walking further.

As we walk toward the elementary school, Lakeyna said, "Can we go to Eddie's and get snacks on credit, Coley?"

Eddie's was a family-run neighborhood grocery store located on Imperial. Most of the low-income single parents went there to shop on credit until the first of the month, when they receive their welfare checks. Then they would pay Eddie back his money and start all over again for the next month.

I would shortcut through the alley to get there from home sometimes. I usually didn't mind stopping by the store when I had money, which was very rare. Sometimes, I would push my luck and try to get my own credit on my mom's tab.

It wouldn't always work, because the bill would be high already, plus Eddie knows that when I come for Mom, it was usually with a note with her signature on it for me to get cigarettes. It's still crazy how they would sell me cigarettes just like that back then.

"Mom already owe Eddie, Keyna, I tried getting some pads yesterday and he barely let me." Any time I didn't have pads when I was on my period (and mine started when I was just 11), I would have to use a sock and wrap tissue around it if there was any. The worst was that I bled heavy for a little skinny girl who only weighed about 100 pounds and had the worst cramps ever. I hated getting blood on the side of my panties, but it happened constantly.

I was thankful Eddie let me get pads that day, the ones with wings that made me feel secure.

Other times, when I would go to the nurse's office crying about my cramps, and they would only give me three or four pads. I would make sure I stop by there before I went home in order to have enough to last me through the night.

I explained to Lakeyna that we could only buy things when Mom gets her welfare check and pays him back. But Keyna didn't understand.

She just knew she was hungry, and she wanted a snack, that's it. Keyna was a fussy eater for a kid who didn't have much. She didn't like meat on the bone and she really didn't eat too much of anything. She only loved noodles, chips, and juice.

She began to cry because there were no snacks, and they couldn't eat cereal because there wasn't any of that left either. I felt like shit. I didn't have anything to give her to stop her from crying. "Keyna, I'm trying to get you to school early enough so you can go eat breakfast. Make sure you eat all your lunch at school, okay? So, you won't be hungry later." I calmly tried to console her.

Since my mom was on welfare, we got lunch cards, which meant free breakfast and lunch from the county every day. The food wasn't that great, but it did the job. For me, it was super embarrassing when you go through the free lunch line in high school, which means you're poor, and I would try and leave class early to be the first in line so that anyone won't see me.

Keyna smudges her tears across her face and sadly says, "Okay, Coley."

"If you stop crying, I promise I'll get you some snacks when you get home from school. Everything will be okay, so stop crying now."

Lakeyna says again in her whiny voice, "Okay, Coley."

"I love you guys, I'll see you later," I say, kissing them on the foreheads. We're at the school now, and I watch them leave before crossing the street to get the school myself.

Entering Lincoln High School from the back gate, I spotted my friends Aaliyah and Sa'adha down the field.

Sometimes, Aaliyah and Sa'adha would walk with me to drop my sisters off at school. They both lived in the same apartments across the street from mine. But this particular morning, I was probably running late or something. I can't remember, but they had left before me.

"Hey, what's up. What time y'all get here?" I ask.

Aaliyah replies, "Hey, Coley. About ten minutes ago. You dropped your sisters off at school already?"

"Girl, yes, had to drop them off."

Sa'adha greets me now with a hug, "Hey, girl, what it doo," while grabbing me and hugging me.

These two friends always made me feel loved. They didn't know what exactly I was going through since I never shared it, and my mom was never mean to my friends that she liked, and they loved her too. I avoided bringing them around anytime I knew she was high. I didn't want them to get a different perception of her.

We walk up to the quad together before the first bell rings.

Later that day, at lunchtime, I meet Sa'adha at the Taco Bell stand by the cafeteria.

Sa'adha says when she sees me, "Hey, Boo, you want a burrito?"

"Hell yeah! I'm starving!" Free lunch was never enough for me, because I can eat, but I stayed hungry.

Sa'adha laughs as she buys the burrito and buys herself a pizza.

Food in hand, we found a bench to sit and start girl talking. I really can't remember how the conversation got brought up, all I know is, she was in love with this dude named Jabez, and she heard some girls from our school had gone over to his house.

I later came to find out one of the girls happened to be my cousin Faas, who was very pretty. Our senior year, she won "most attractive" in our yearbook superlatives. Well, Sa'adha was hot, venting her feelings and emotions and how upset she was about Faas stepping on her toes. I was a good friend to vent to. I was a good listener when it came to drama, probably because it wasn't mine for once.

Sa'adha tells me, "Jabez called me last night. He wants to come over tomorrow, and I really want to see him to see what's up and what's going on. You wanna come with me?" she asks. "His best friend Farrell is going to be there, and he told me to bring a homegirl if I can."

Is this the same Farrell everybody has been talking about around here? I wonder. I had heard his name while walking to math class last week, and I had seen a picture that my cousin Taguhi had. It was ripped from girls trying to snatch it, and I could barely see what he looked like. From the little I did see; he didn't look bad. I was curious about what everybody was going crazy over. I wouldn't mind meeting this Farrell in person.

But instead, I say, "Girl, you know I ain't ever ditched school. My mom will kill me if she finds out. Plus, I got to pick up my sisters. Tomorrow is their early day."

"Come on, girl, grow some balls. You never did nothing; your mom won't find out. I need someone to come with me, I don't want to go by myself. We will be back in enough time to get your sisters. We will only go for a little while. I just want to go see Jabez really quick."

"Okay, are you sure?" I ask, second-guessing myself. I wanted to see why all these girls were going looney and spreading Farrell's name all around our school, like he's the king of Lincoln when he didn't even attend Lincoln. I didn't know if he was worth risking getting killed for. But Sa'adha assured me she had skipped school before and made it back, no problem.

"Yes, I've done it before, girl. Stop tripping, we gone be good, I promise you!"

This was dumb, and I knew it. Her mom won't murder her if she gets caught. I wasn't even thinking about Farrell before she brought him to my attention. I would just listen to girls talk about him like it had nothing to do with me. Now, suddenly, I couldn't wait to see him. That was peer pressure.

"Okay, girl, I'll be ready," I said, though I was still not too sure about the situation.

The whole night, I couldn't sleep. I was up pondering, thinking if I should go or not. In the end, I talked myself into it. It was time to go out on a limb. Forget the rules, Sa'adha was right, I never did nothing up until this point.

The next morning, I woke up ready to go. I turned on the radio to my favorite song by Destiny Child, "Say My Name," and stared in the mirror, acting like I was Kelly Rowland herself. My adrenaline was racing. I never ditched school in my life. I was turned all the way up!

I didn't have many clothes, but I made sure I found my best pair of shoes for that day, which were some red Saucony's, and my cleanest outfit, which was my cousin Vadimir's red Fubu sweater that she let me borrow and I never returned. Then I paired it with blue jeans in a style that came to my ankles. I was feeling confident because my cousin Dada had done cornrows for me a few nights before. I was looking attractive. No bald ponytail today, boo. Here I come!

I was feeling good, like everything was meant to be and nothing could bring me down. I didn't care if my mom woke up mad, yelling out of her codeine coma over whatever she was going through. Forget that! I raced to get my sisters dressed and get ready to get out of here.

I rushed my sisters to school so fast that you would have thought I was a Tasmanian devil. I wanted to hurry up and find Sa'adha.

Before we go, let me fill you in on my girl Sa'adha. She was pretty to me, beautiful black skin, long legs, and white teeth. She ran track, played basketball, and dressed cute.

Her apartment was always the best apartment on the block. She lived in two different ones, and on the inside, her place was nice. Both her parents were around, and she had two younger brothers and an older sister. I would say she was a little bit more promiscuous than I was, probably because she had an older sister with a baby.

I loved her sister, Sara, and her daughter was very pretty, too. I looked at Sara like a big sister and I loved being around her. I would be hungry and she would let me eat at her house. She was the first person to make me a grilled cheese sandwich with syrup on top of it. Their place was like a real home.

Not like mine. My mom got kicked off Section 8 for failing her inspection and for not staying on top of things. When we were living in Bayview Heights, my mom would leave me with the neighbor her friend Ms. Yvonne and big Jar and their two sons that I looked at like brothers and go out to meet Navy men. This was before my sisters were born.

I remember one night, she had this man Jeff over, and I guess she had said or done something that made him mad, because I woke up and saw him grabbing her head and putting it through the wall. I went back to my room and acted like I hadn't seen it, because I didn't know what to do to help her.

She also had a sugar daddy at this time named Candy Man that was married. He loved my mom's dirty draws. When I say I didn't want for anything back then, believe me. When he was around, there is nothing I wanted for.

I remember waking up one Christmas morning to so many presents under the tree. It was everything a kid could want. You name it, from bikes to Nintendo's, it was all for me. My mom was working at the Eazy-8 hotel in La Mesa at the time, and I knew she couldn't afford all that alone.

He bought my mom her first and only car, a red four-door Escort, brand new and shiny. Their relationship lasted for a few years, and then he died. My mom took that hard, even though she was dating Keyna's dad at the same time. Not too long after that, she ended up pregnant with my sister.

I didn't really know Rafael, my sister Keyna's dad, that well at all. I knew he was in the Navy and from a different state. He was always back and forth. He was a handsome guy. I knew my mom was in love with him, but I don't think the feeling was mutual. I was young, but I still took him as a guy that had lots of kids and women all over the country.

I remember waking up one night looking for my mom and when I found her, she was on the couch with Rafael, sucking his dick. I did not like him after that. I thought he was using my mom for sex and to have somewhere to stay while he was in San Diego. I believe he is part of the reason why I harbored resentment towards men.

The things I saw certainly skewed my views back then. I started humping on my girl cousins' young when we would playhouse. I would always want to be the dad while they would play the mom. I would suck on their titties and everything, really trying to play the man's role. It was odd, I know, but we were young, impressionable, and surrounded by dysfunction.

Around 1990

I recall Rafael being an alcoholic, wrecking my mom's car and totaling it out. He didn't help her get another one or anything.

He ended up going back to wherever he came from. I don't remember ever seeing him after that, until months after Keyna was born. I remember his mom showing up with him. He stayed for a few months, then had to go back overseas. He was gone for something like a year.

By the time Rafael came back around, my mom had moved on with Trice dad, Maartje. He was younger than my mom by ten years. One Easter Sunday, we went to Emerald Hills Park looking to meet up with him and a few of my mom's homegirls.

That was my first time being in a shooting. That was around the same time Mom stopped caring about things. I think her addiction had started taking over her to a great extent.

That was when I realized that Candy Man would supply my mom with the pills. She would never have to buy them because he made sure she was straight. Her money didn't go toward the pills back then because he was the pill man himself, but once he died, she had to start supplying them herself, and she struggled.

While my mom was pregnant with Latrice, I was thinking to myself, I was not ready for all this. Lakeyna was still a baby, and I was the one really taking care of her and I was only 10. I wanted a sister, but two, and back-to-back — that is a lot.

Around that time, we ended up moving to East Diego on 50th Street. Living there was alright, except Maartje ended up moving in with us.

I was not used to a man living with us, and it started getting annoying because he and my mom would fight constantly like cats and dogs. Then Latrice was born on June 6, 1993. She was a blessing, and by then, I was over the fact of having to care for two babies. I was in love with her and I was willing to do what it took to take care of her.

Shortly after my sister was born, we had to move again, downgrade to something my mom could afford. We stayed in that apartment for about a year. Part of the problem was that Maartje didn't work or help my mom with anything. That's where most of their arguments came from. Part of me felt bad watching my mom struggle, but I thought, what did she expect? That's how she got him.

We moved on to Imperial and 50th Street, and Maartje ended up moving in with his grandfather. His grandfather's house was around the corner on Manomet, in Lincoln Park. I loved his grandfather, or Poppy as we called him. He was a nice man. Plus, I was happy Maartje wasn't living with us anymore. We lived in the 50th Street apartment until we moved with Auntie Jackie, and I hated it.

Don't get me wrong. I lived in the most raggedy apartments on the block. Our apartment was cramped and not so clean. That's the first time I ever saw a rat. When I saw that hairy thing crawling across the floor, I cried, "Mom, there are rats here," and she just screamed at the top of her lungs back at me, "That isn't no damn rat, that's a mouse!" I kept looking at her thinking, what's the difference? Both were disgusting.

It was bad there, and it got to a point where I was stealing mice traps, trying to catch them myself.

I would wake up in the morning with two or three mice on a sticky trap. I would toss the trap out the window like it was a Frisbee, watching the mice fly away like they were on an airborne carnival ride.

We didn't have screens in the window, so it was easy access to throw them out. After a while, I looked forward to Frisbeeing them out the window. I wasn't scared of them anymore.

By the time I was eleven, I thought I was a professional thief. I got tired of being hungry and my mom not worried about anything unless it had to do with her fix. She was selfish, and that's what addiction does to you. You stop caring about anything or anyone else. She would give me a list of things to go steal from the store for her.

She sent me to the 99-cent store one day and I got caught trying to put the last pack of crackers in my backpack. Luckily, the lady at the counter didn't call the police, just told me to put them back and get out of the store. When I got home, my mom got mad at me for not bringing the crackers back, and she made me go to another store to go get the things I wasn't able to get.

She was a cold piece of work.

Anytime she let me, I would go to Sa'adha's apartment to try and escape my mom and everything going on at home. My friends didn't know I was stealing food. I was very discrete about all the stuff I was doing, and I was too embarrassed and afraid I would get clowned if anyone knew. It was bad enough that I was already getting clowned for things that I couldn't hide.

Sa'adha's apartment was always fun, and my homeboys Nabil Aamir lived nearby as well. I would be at their houses often, too, and their moms loved me. Aamir's mom Ms. Jacira loved me so much that she would tell me that she wanted me to marry her son when we grew up. She and Nabil's mom Ms. Aamu were friends of my mom as well. I adored them like they were my blood aunties. They were my favorite people on 50th street.

If I wasn't in their apartments, we were all on the green box in front of my apartment. My little cousin Boo hung with us too, until I had to go into the house.

I would always be the first to get called in. It would often still be light outside and I hated having to go so soon. I would have to go attend to my sisters. Boo, my cousin, lived in the same apartments as me, but he always got to stay out late. Boo would go to the skating rink, and he always had money, nice clothes, and his mom had a job. I could not stand him at times. She would even let girls come over to their house. He was sexually active early, and he got to do everything, maybe because he was a boy, I was jealous of Boo.

I could never do any of that. Not saying I wanted to have sex. I just wanted to be a kid so bad. I would get so upset that he was much younger than me but got to do anything and everything he wanted. He had a smart mouth. All he would do was talk back. He never had to do chores or anything around the house. If you ask him to take out the trash, he'd already be going crazy. He was that spoiled.

Around 1999

It's lunch time, the day we're supposed to go see Jabez and Farrell, and here comes Sa'adha. "Hey, boo, you ready?" she says with a wicked smile.

"Oh my God, I'm nervous. Let's go! Let's get this over with," I reply.

We began walking to the number 11 bus stop that will take us to Farrell's house. My heart is racing, hoping none of my mom's friends or family would see me. She knows everyone in Southeast because it's a small part of the town. When we got on the bus, I confess to Sa'adha how nervous I am. How was she so used to something like this, I asked, and she just laughed.

As the bus rolled on, I loosened up a little bit. The funny conversation we were having helped, and it made the ride go fast. Before too long, we made it to our destination: Skyline.

Immediately when we arrived, my adrenaline began racing again. Being a girl from Lincoln High School, every girl from Morse High School, which was in Skyline, pretty much hated us. Our two schools were like rival gangs. We were in enemy territory, and we really didn't have no business being over there, period.

We walk a short way to Farrell's house. When we arrive, Sa'adha knocks. A boy answers the door. "What's up, Sa'adha? Where have you been, girl?"

"Hey, Farrell, what's up?" she smiles and hugs him. "The last time I came around, you weren't here," she said in her cute voice.

"Jabez ain't here," he tells us, "But y'all welcome to come in and wait for him. He should be back soon; blood didn't tell me where he was going." They always called each other "blood" as a show of allegiance.

"What? Jabez ain't here?" With her attitude, voice, and straight face, Sa'adha plays it real cool. "Where is he? He knew I was coming. Come on Coley," she gestures to me. We walk in and sit on the couch.

Farrell eyes me and says, "You're not going to introduce me to your friend?"

Sa'adha doesn't care. She has an attitude because Jabez wasn't there, so I have to introduce myself. "Hi, I'm Lacole."

Farrell smiles, "What's up Lacole?"

I smile back and wave, acting like I had never heard of him in my life. "Hey, Farrell, nice to meet you." He does look as good as everyone had been saying to me. He was about 5'7, real dark smooth skin, waves on his head, and his teeth and lips are big. He had a gap in between his two front teeth, but they were white. He had a nice smile. He was sexy! He introduces himself as GF the great. When he says that, Sa'adha and I both start laughing.

Farrell ask, "What's so funny?"

"What's so great about you?" I ask. "And what does GF stand for?"

"Great Farrell, and there's only one way to find out..." he replies, and his smile finishes for him. "Y'all straight ditching stinking Lincoln today, huh? To come see us?"

"I guess, if that's what you want to call it," Sa'adha says, still bent out of shape.

From there, Farrell starts joking, and me and Sa'adha are laughing hard enough to burst. She loosens up. He's clearly a clown, super funny with a great sense of humor, and a cool personality too. I began enjoying his company.

"Jabez should be here soon. Y'all wanna go in my room and listen to music? I got the slaps," Farrell offers.

I ask him, "What kind of music you listen to?"

"A little bit of everything, Jagged Edge, Mack Dre, Keith the Sneak, and Messy Marv. What are you looking for, baby?" and flashes that smile again.

When we get to his room, we sit on Farrell's bed. He turns on the music, and we ask to look at his yearbook and pictures we see on his dresser. He hands them to us. I notice a picture of a mixed girl with long hair. She looks Filipino and black, from where I'm sitting, and she is pretty. Her picture is one of the photos on his dresser, standing up. I think maybe she is someone important. There aren't too many pictures on the dresser. I ask him who she is, and he replies that she's a friend named Chantey.

He asks us if we want anything to drink, then gets up to get us waters. We sit there for almost thirty minutes, listening to music and looking at pictures, and joking as well. Then the doorbell rings and in comes the darkest guy I've ever seen in my life. He has a slicked-up perm, hair going back, and it is not attractive at all. He enters the room.

"What's up, pretty ladies? What's up with y'all?" He introduces himself as Ice, while reaching out his hands for a handshake.

Sa'adha says, "My name is Tasha, Jebez's girl." She shakes his hand, but her face says shut up, ugly, and stop talking to me.

I have a big smirk on my face; I know Sa'adha. "Hi, I'm Lacole."

Ice keeps talking, "That's what's up! Where y'all pretty ladies coming from?"

"We go to Lincoln," I say. Sa'adha looks at me to say, shut up, you are volunteering too much information.

But I didn't know. This was my first time at this, and I'm just trying to be friendly.

"Wow, Lincoln!" He looks at Farrell with a surprise on his face, like us being there was wrong. We went to Lincoln, and girls that went to Lincoln were a no because they think we might set them up.

Farrell tells him, "They bool, blood." Being bloods, they say "bool" instead of "cool," just for the sound.

You can tell that Ice thought we'd might have set them up. Farrell probably paged him and told him to come to the house because we were there.

"You sure, blood?" he says.

Farrell gives Ice a gang handshake. "What's up, blood?" he says, emphasizing blood.

Seeming satisfied, Ice comes in and sits on the floor. Then he started looking at the yearbook with us. Farrell shows us Ice's picture in the yearbook, and he starts clowning him. It goes from there and they start clowning each other, and me and Sa'adha can't help but laugh.

Farrell and Ice start talking about a situation that occurred the night before. Then Ice asks Farrell if he wants to smoke a blunt.

"Blood, you know we can't smoke in here. We must go to your house. Jabez's mom will be here any minute from now. I think she went to the store."

Farrell's dad and his wife had moved out of town and left his house to Jabez's mom, who let Farrell stay with them. Jabez and Farrell were close. He didn't want to move out of town with his dad. My opinion? He was too sucked into the gang banging lifestyle and wanted to do him. He was able to make that choice, being over 18. Besides, Jabez's mom loved Farrell, she didn't have a problem with his decision.

Farrell turns to me and Sa'adha. "Y'all wanna walk down to Ice's with us so we can smoke this blunt and wait for Jabez?"

We look at each other shrug our shoulders, realizing we ain't got nothing else to do. We really didn't want to leave. We just got there, plus Sa'adha wanted to see her man. That was the whole point of us ditching school and coming all this way.

So, we're walking to Ice's house. Farrell and Ice are telling jokes and Sa'adha and I are busting up. These dudes are funny! I'm loving Farrell's sense of humor and personality. I see why he's a lady's man. I'm not showing any signs that I like him though. That's not part of the plan.

I really hadn't thought I would be feeling him so soon like this. I had only planned to go see what he looked like in person and keep Sa'adha company, that's all.

But it'd been less than an hour, and I was already falling for him. I was never fast to give it away. I wasn't the type of girl that liked attention from guys. I didn't even like wearing shorts. And if I liked a guy, he would never be able to tell.

We arrive at Ice's house. It took us about two minutes to get there. We are standing in the garage and he asks if we want to take a seat on the sofa that was in there. Sa'adha hesitates. She doesn't want to get too comfortable; she really didn't even want to go down there. She is thinking about Jabez and getting back. I just followed suit.

Ice isn't the best-looking guy, but he knows how to treat the ladies. I know now why his name is Ice: he looks like he could put out a fire with his skin. He's cool though, and he makes me feel comfortable at his house, regardless of whether we are standing or sitting.

Farrell tells him, "Fire it up, blood," emphasis on blood once again.

Ice offers it to us, "Y'all smoke?" No, we don't.

Sa'adha asks Farrell, "Where is Jabez? Call him. I'm ready to go."

Farrell replies, "Sa'adha, we just got here. Can I finish the blunt? I'm trying to get high. Your bool, he's coming. Hopefully, he will be there by the time we get back. You gone get to see that Negro, so calm down."

Sa'adha doesn't like being told to calm down. "Shut up, Farrell. Call Jabez. He's taking way too long, and we have to leave by 12:30. I didn't come over here to see you and Ice smoke in the garage."

Farrell says coolly, "Alright, you serious about yours."

They finish the blunt, and we start walking back to the house, hoping Jabez is back, or at least on his way back. Farrell's back to being humorous. I guess this is him all day, every day. He is too good at it.

Sa'adha tells him, "Shut up Farrell, you always clowning," but she's laughing happily while we walk back.

Farrell doesn't stop. "You know me," he says, "I stay with the jokes," and he's cracking up again with his big white teeth.

Sa'adha says suddenly, "Why you take us to your ugly friend's house?"

Farrell's tone turns serious but still joking. "Blood, that's messed up you are clowning the homie like that. I'm going to tell blood you wanna holler at him next time."

"No, the hell you not," Sa'adha shoots back with a serious face, rolling her eyes. "I'm telling Jabez you said that"

"Blood isn't tripping, he knows he isn't no threat."

Meanwhile, I'm dying laughing. Everybody says I'm super goofy and it doesn't take much to make me laugh. I'm always laughing, even though my teeth are chipped from when I was younger playing kickball.

I was a tomboy. I liked hanging out with the boys doing rough stuff. Joe, Sam, Big Boy Tee, my cousin Boo, and probably a few others were all out playing that time. I remember I was running toward the ball to kick it, but somehow, someway, the ball rolled up underneath my foot and my foot came down right on top of it. And that's all she wrote. I remember doing the splits, and my face hitting the ground, and next thing I remember I'm tasting blood.

My mom was pissed off when I came in the house, mouth bleeding, and my teeth were chipped. I almost got another whooping for chipping my own teeth on accident. I had just got a whooping the day before for getting caught in the canyon with red ants all over me. This was all before my sisters were born, before my mom fell into her addiction. If she was already on pills, I could never tell. She was always on point. She kept her hair done, wore cute outfits, and all the man liked her.

She would make sure I looked cute right along with her back then.

We continue to wait on Jabez in Farrell's room, listening to music on his twin-size bed that can barely fit all of us.

When Jabez finally arrives, he looks much older than I expected. He is cute and dressed nice, but I didn't realize he was so much older than Sa'adha.

Sa'adha is over the moon to see him. She jumps off the bed and leaves the room so fast she didn't even look back. Now, it's me and Farrell alone. He changes the mood and turns on "Let's Get Married" by Jagged Edge. That's my song; I don't know what his intentions were, so I'm playing it cool, chilling.

He starts asking all these questions. Who am I dating? What's my boyfriend's name? Do I ever hear his name around school? He's trying to find out everything he can about himself and what goes on around our school.

I filled him in about this boy named Tanu, who's been in love with me since 9th grade. We used to be in the same English class together before I got placed in Special Ed. He would give me the answers to our work for a kiss sometimes. He was a football player and a lot of girls liked him. He was an immensely popular guy.

He would tell me things like I was the prettiest girl in the whole school. That was very flattering to me, because of everything I was going through. Everyone knew he liked me, and he wanted to date me. My brother Reg and my best friend Pat would stay making jokes about it to me.

Tenth grade year homecoming was the first dance I ever went to. I didn't have a date. My mom said I could go, but not with a boy, so I went with Aaliyah.

Tanu was there, and he was happy to see me. He was there with his friends too. He asked if I would take a picture with him. I remember taking the picture and him putting his hand on my butt.

He brings a copy of the picture to school for me a few days later. I'm scared to show my mom, and it took me a few weeks to work up the guts. When I finally did show her, she liked it. I was surprised she didn't say anything about him having his hand on my butt.

As we got older, I could tell Tanu still had that desire for me. Lots of people thought he was mean, but he was sweet to me. I don't know why we never got together. Kissing was as far as we went. He was always a gentleman to me.

Instead of him, I started talking to this boy named Ranson. That turned out to be a disaster. He had too much going on as a young boy; he even went to jail. I don't know why I ever liked him.

While we were together, he started cheating on me with this other girl. I wasn't sexually active, but she was. She was ghetto. She started calling my phone, wanting to fight me and everything. I heard she had gotten pregnant with his baby, even though he was saying it wasn't true.

Not only that, but he also had a girlfriend who lived by him and went to another school. She was pretty. He was dating her before me and before the pregnant girl.

I found out about all this from one of my friends Jaasau, who was dating my big cousin Taisito. The pretty girl happened to be her best friend, and she was basically letting me know what was up.

I had no business even talking to Ranson. My cousin Taisito had already warned me about him. He said he didn't want me dating none of his friends. They were all bad news, he said. I didn't want my cousin to be mad at me, so I would sneak around and talk to him from time to time.

After I found out about all the lies, I wasn't feeling Ranson no longer. When he calls, I make up things so I don't even have to deal with him. If i could just change my number so he couldn't reach me, I would do just that. He doesn't go to my school anymore; he doesn't go to any school. He probably was thinking we're still together. If I had it my way, I wouldn't see Ranson ever again.

I tell Farrell he looks at me, surprised. "Taisito, that's your cousin? I know blood, that's crazy."

"I hope you know my cousin Taisito in a good way. That's my favorite boy cousin."

"I don't think he would approve of you talking to me either," he laughs out loud.

"Why are you laughing?" I demand. He ignores the question.

"I know Tanu, too." He's shaking his head with a smirk on his face. "You sure you never dated Tanu?"

"How do you know Tanu?"

Farrell says, "We go way back, we played football together. Your cousin is cool. You don't have nothing to worry about. Tell him you came over here and see what he says."

I simply say, "Good," rolling my eyes and neck with a look that says, please don't ask me no more questions about my school or my homies, especially my cousin. I didn't come here for that, and I don't know what he was trying to find out. I just came to support my friend and to see what everybody loves so much about this Mr. Farrell

But the questions don't stop. Now he wants to know where I live, who I live with, what I like to do for fun, how old I am, what grade am I in…

I feel like we're playing a game of 21 questions. "Are you feeling me or something?" I ask, laughing out loud. "You are getting really personal."

Farrell shrugs and says casually, "I'm trying to get to know you, see who you are as a person and to see if we are vibing or not. You are cute though."

"Thanks," I say, nervous from the seductive look he gave me as he said that last part. I open some. "Nah, I can't never do anything. I have no hobbies, no free time. I live with my mom on 50th & Imperial, right across the street from Lincoln High.

"My Dad's in prison. I have two younger sisters that I must take care of every day. So, you probably won't ever see me again. This is my first-time ditching school and honestly, I'm scared. I hope and pray my mom doesn't find out, otherwise, my ass is grass." I had no problem telling him that my mom beats me.

"How old are your little sisters?"

"Latrice is five, Lakeyna is six. Are we finished with the questions? Not trying to be rude, but enough of me."

"I guess you don't really like talking too much, huh?"

I ignore him and try to go around the question. What I really wanted to say is, it's not that I don't like talking. I just don't know what his motive is, but I really don't know him like that to share all my personal business.

I didn't like talking about my personal business to just anyone. I was embarrassed. I just didn't know how to say it without him thinking I was being rude.

I'm starting to get hot in his room. I had on a sweater with a white shirt underneath. He had closed the door when Sa'adha went out, it had gotten stuffy real fast in that small room. I didn't know if I was hot from all the questions or what.

Here I was, in the room with a cute older boy, alone. My nose sweats a lot when I'm nervous. My forehead was even sweating bullets. My mom would say my nose would sweat because I'm evil. My dad sweats a lot, and I think I inherited it from him.

Farrell looks at me and say, "Your nose is sweating. If you're hot, take your sweater off."

"I'm good, my nose always sweats during rain, sleet or snow, even if it's cold outside, it doesn't matter."

"You sure you don't want me to go get the fan?"

"That'll be cool, thanks for offering," I say, relieved.

Eventually, I can't take it anymore. My sweater must come off. The fan isn't getting the job done.

Farrell is sitting awfully close to me, making me worry. He starts kissing me on my cheek and rubbing my back. I don't know what to do next. I am so nervous.

I loosen up I was relaxed by my back being rub, and things start feeling right. He kisses me on the lips now. I look him in his sexy face and kiss his lips back while grabbing his chin. From there, he lays me on my back on his bed and starts kissing me in a very sensual way. Rubbing my face, looking me in my eyes, kissing my nose, rubbing his ears on my cheeks telling me how cute I was.

Then he gets on top of me. We are grinding with our clothes on. He starts trying to feel my titties through my bra, then lifts my hands up to take my undershirt off. From there, everything on the top is off. He is sucking my nipples slowly while caressing my titties.

My panties are wet. He's unfastening my pants. "Farrell wait," I say. "What are you doing? We don't even know each other like that. I literally met you a few hours ago."

Farrell growls low, "I want to eat you out. Have you ever been eaten out before? Are you gone let me? Let me be the first."

I don't say anything, but I'm thinking to myself, hell yeah. I ain't never had this done before by somebody that I wanted to do it. He got big juicy lips too. In my head, I'm asking him to please hurry up and go down.

Enough talking, I'm horny now. I don't protest.

I continued letting him do him. He had no intentions on eating it. He just said that to get my pants down. As soon as he gets them down, he notices how soaked my panties are and sticks it straight in.

No condom, no nothing. It hurt so bad. I was moaning so loud. He whispers in my ear, "Hold on, baby, this feeling is amazing. This is the best I have ever had in my life. I don't want to come out."

I think to myself, how many girls have you had.

It doesn't take long for him to finish his business. Just minutes maybe. I am happy it was fast because the whole time I was in pain. I didn't know what to think. My vagina is bleeding, hurting, and it feels swollen. It didn't feel good to me one bit. All I can think about now is pregnancy, STDs, my mom and how I didn't even know this boy.

He got the best of me. I start putting on my clothes, crying in a state of shock. At this point, what was done was done. All I can do is go.

"What's wrong baby? Why are you crying?"

"Do you know what you just did to me?" I demand, staring him in the eyes.

Farrell is laughing, thinking everything is a joke, saying, "You got that good."

"What do you mean? What's wrong with you? I don't even know you. I just had sex with you and I feel horrible. Please, can you go get Sa'adha for me. I'm ready to go" I say to Farrell. I feel real low right now.

Farrell doesn't move. He says, "I didn't think it was that serious, you started kissing back. I thought you were feeling me like I was feeling you."

"Of course, you don't think it's that serious. You probably do this all the time, with any girl whatsoever. Leave me alone!"

Farrell retorts, "I don't do this all the time when girls come over. You think I just be giving this dick away?"

"Yep, pretty much," I snap back, not wanting to hear anything he has to say

I walk out the room fast, irritated about what I had just done. Farrell follows me. I'm calling Sa'adha's name, ready to go.

I'm not wanting to hate on her program, but I don't want to stay around any longer. I feel humiliated, plus it is almost time for school to get out. We must get back to the other side of town, and soon. My sisters get out of school early today. I can't be late picking them up or my mom will really know I was up to something.

When Sa'adha sees my upset face, she immediately asks, "What's wrong? Are you okay? Farrell, what did you do to my friend?" She's rolling her neck and asking what happened.

Probably the look on my face gave it away. I try not to make a big deal of it though. "Yea, I'm good, I'm just ready to go. You ready?"

But Sa'adha won't let it go so easily. "Farrell, let me find out you did something to my friend..." she threatens.

"Y'all leaving already? I didn't do nothing, I promise you. I like Lacole, I don't know why she's tripping. Talk to your girl, I swear," he says, throwing his hands up innocently.

I'm rolling my eyes, "Let's go." She kisses Jabez bye, telling him she'll call him later. We started walking to the bus stop. Farrell walks with us and offers to drop us off back at the school. All I want is him far away from me. All that joking isn't even working at this point. I don't want no ride or anything, we are getting back on the bus just like we came. I just don't want Sa'adha to notice me acting weird toward him.

Soon as we got on the bus, I let it all out, filling Sa'adha in about everything that happened.

I can tell Sa'adha thought I was going to say something totally different. She looked surprised, like maybe she thought I was overreacting, but you can tell she felt bad for me though.

She calms me down and let me know it wasn't that bad. Everything would be okay. And she reminds me that I let it happen, which was true. I guess I was just in the moment. I don't know why I was so mad at myself.

We arrive back at Lincoln High. I walk across the street to get my sisters from school. "Hey, Keyna and Trice, how was your day? Did you guys eat all your lunch today?"

"Yes, Coley, we had a good day, and we ate all our food," Trice answers.

Then Keyna asks, "Coley, you got our snacks? You said that you were going to get snacks for us. I want my hot Cheetos."

I tell her, "I'm going to drop you off at home with Mom, then go get them for you, okay? I promise."

"Okay," Keyna says excitedly. "Thank you, Coley."

I'm walking home holding Keyna's hand on one side and Trice's hand in my other, thinking to myself what I'm going to steal from the grocery store. My sisters are hungry. I promised Keyna I was getting them snacks, but we owe Eddie already for the credit last month and we don't have anything at home.

First, I drop my sisters off at home with my mom. When we arrive, she is in the shower. I empty my backpack and go out again, down the street to Food 4 Less, off Euclid and Imperial.

I fill my backpack up with whatever I can get my hands on that will fit and let it still zip up. The only thing I smash is the bread, since it's still edible that way and will still serve its purpose.

When I get home, Mom starts going off on me immediately. "Where yo ass been? Why you drop the girls off and didn't say shit and walk your ass out this house like you grown, bitch? You are not grown, and next time you walk your ass out this house, you make sure you take your sisters with you. I don't know who the fuck you think you are—"

I cut her off. "Mom, I went to the store to steal some food. I didn't want to take Keyna and Trice, they would have slowed me down. I didn't want to risk getting caught with them."

Mom softens, "Okay, thanks, baby. What did you get from the store? I hope you got some bread."

I empty my backpack out and show her the slightly squished loaf. I put the rest of the food away and prepare to make my sisters something to eat. I know they are starving.

Mom gives me a look, like I done good. How was I supposed to think stealing isn't normal when my own mom is okay with it?

"Lacole, did you happen to leave school today?" she asks suddenly.

"No, why would you ask me that, Mom? Why would I leave school?" I'm trying hard to stay calm, but my heart is racing.

"Well, why the hell did the damn school leave a message saying you missed six and seventh period?" she asks, crossing her arms.

"I do not know, Mom. I was at school all day. You can ask Sa'adha and Aaliyah, they were with me." I prayed this would be the end of it, but Mom was just getting started.

"Bitch, let me find out you are ditching school, I'll beat your ass. Are you fucking, Lacole? I'm going to take your ass to Planned Parenthood to find out if you are fucking or not, put your ass on some birth control pills. We have no room for no kids around here, you already got your sisters to take care of."

Inside, I hope and pray that's not possible. I'm scared right now. I hope Mom really doesn't find out if I ditched school today. That will for sure be a good beating. My mom doesn't play. She might be little, but she has a big woman's complex.

Later that night, the phone rings. It's Farrell. I forgot I gave this boy my number before we had sex. I pick up and hear Farrell says, "Can I speak to Cole?"

"Yea, this is her. Who's this?" I ask, even though I know it's him. I know his voice, and not too many other boys have my number. I feel like giving him a hard time. "What's up, Farrell? What do you want?"

"Damn, what, you mean you still mad about what happened earlier? Did you talk to your homegirl Sa'adha?"

"No, I haven't. Why do you care if we talked or not? What do you want? Am I not supposed to be mad anymore? You act like what happened was a long time ago. do you remember what happened today? I had sex with you and I don't even know you."

He responds, "Yes, I loved it and I'll never forget it. I don't see the problem. That's why I'm calling you, maybe we can get to know each other. I was trying to get to know you today, but time was short and you really didn't like talking about yourself that much. I didn't want to force you to talk. Now, I'm thinking it's probably a better time for you, at least I'm hoping. You seemed to be under a lot of pressure earlier.

"Is there anything you want to ask me that you didn't get to ask me today? I don't care what it is, if it's personal, whatever. You got my undivided attention, Cole. I like you. For that reason, you seem different to me.

"I don't know if it's because you started crying after we had sex or what, but you're starting to make me feel bad. No one has ever done that to me. Now, it is our time to get to know each other. You okay with that?"
"I'm still mad," I tell him, "And even if you don't see anything wrong with today, I didn't like it none of it. It was a horrible experience, it hurt, and I regret every bit of it now.

I feel it's a big problem and I don't feel like talking about anything right now. I'll call you back another day when I'm over it."

Farrell is not to be dissuaded. "Well, maybe we can do it again next time and we can see if it's better. As a matter of fact, I'll make sure you like it next time. Tell me how you like it, and you got it."

I could tell he was smiling while saying it, and that just makes me angrier. "Really? You say all the wrong things. You suck, boy. Bye. There won't be a next time," and I hang up the phone.

He calls back. "Why you hang up, Lacole? That was Hella rude. Your wrong right now with whatever you're thinking."

"I told you, I do not feel like talking right now, Farrell. You aren't going to force me to talk. I'll call you back later."

"How are you going to call me back, Cole? You don't even have my number, I just got yours."

I'm thinking to myself, why is he calling me Cole? I introduced myself as Lacole. He came up with a nickname already. The nerve of this boy.

"Okay then, what's your number, Farrell?" I write down the number as we said our goodbyes.

I really don't know why I'm still so mad at him. After all, it takes two. It's not like he forced me to do anything I didn't want to do. I'm old enough to make my own decisions. I just know, I wasn't feeling the situation and how everything went down.

I'm not going to lie I like the fact that he was chasing me even after he'd already gotten the goodies. He could have easily counted me as just one more girl and moved on. It's not like we really knew each other, and plenty of girls liked him. But he was persistent, and he knew what he wanted.

After playing hard to get long enough, I finally gave in. I called. The more we talked, the more I was really starting to like him as a person. We would talk on the phone until we fell asleep. I hadn't even seen him again since the first time we met.

In our long phone calls, we were really starting to get to know one another. I find out Farrell works right by my school Lincoln High, at Cal Trans right off the 805 Interstate, literally a minute away from my school.

He started to drive by my school every day. He drove a grey hatchback Honda with a dent on the right-side front bumper. He had a 20-inch speaker in his trunk, and you could hear his music bumping from a mile away. He would time it to when he knew I was on my way out the front gate. He would hurriedly park and get out in a rush to give me a hug and kiss. I would rush out there too so I wouldn't miss him. After I saw him, I would go pick up my sisters. I was worried Keyna would tell on me. After a few weeks of this, he was really beginning to impress me. I was really starting to feel him more and more each day.

An older guy who's working, going out of his way for me? Dating him might not be so bad. His attention meant even more to me after he said he could get killed over here, being with the gangs and all. I'm starting to feel special, like I got something that all these other girls don't.

Unfortunately, he had stopped dating his pretty girlfriend who went to Morse High School for me, but he was still with her when he was first chasing me. He confessed they had been together for a few years. He never talked too much about her. I was curious why he cheated on her with me. He told me he wasn't in love with her, but he liked her and she was cool.

It was just a high school thing, he said. Basically, he graduated, and she was still in school, and they'd changed. She was my age.

He also said his dad told him to date a black girl, that those mixed girls get older and they start looking different, but black don't crack.

Not saying that was the reason why they broke up; that's just what he expressed to me. I really felt it did not matter at this point. Knowing they were not together any longer was good enough for me. He said I didn't have anything to worry about, and I trusted him. I had no reason not to. I didn't worry because I had to much other stuff to worry about. If I keep getting this same treatment, I have no concerns.

Over time, Farrell opens up about things that happened in his past, girls who liked him, who would come over and hang out with him and his homeboys. Farrell said the girls would come over in packs and everybody was for anybody. Guys can lie too, just to make it sound good. It's not that I didn't believe him, but one of these girls happened to be my best friend Lamya. I knew she had a crush on him like everyone else did. I didn't care about everyone else, but I did care about her.

The thing about Lamya was, she was one of those girls who liked anybody who paid attention to her. If one guy's not showing her action, she's on to the next. She had dudes, so she's not about to waste her time liking one and getting no play. Lamya left Lincoln High School and started going to Garfield. We really didn't talk as much after that.

Farrell told me he knew Lamya liked him. He said she would always want to come over. He was a cocky little thing, always saying which girls liked him and which girls didn't.

I still really couldn't believe what I didn't know and I was really feeling Farrell. He was my man, period.

Then, shortly before me and Farrell started dating, my mom went to jail. She had been forging doctors' signatures to get prescription pills. Her favorite spot for passing off her forged prescriptions was CVS Pharmacy, on 43rd. The cops picked her up right from that CVS. She was caught in the middle of her act, while Keyna, Trice and my cousin Sue were in the car waiting for her.

I was so mad what the hell was we supposed to do now? I just really didn't understand. How the hell was my mom in jail, leaving her three kids at home with no adult around? What part of the game was this? This was something else.

I knew my mom was worse off than she had ever been. She'd been in jail once before this, not too long ago. Now, she was so deep in her addiction that the pills weren't even doing the job anymore. She had started doing crystal meth with this fat man named Tony I hated Tony. He was my uncle's friend from when they were growing up. He lived on the coast; I remember him coming over late at night when we were asleep. I would wake up to go the bathroom and it would smell so bad in there. I knew it wasn't a normal smell. It got to the point where my mom started being so careless or just so high, she left the burned pipe lying around a few times.

I was taking care of the house for about a month for the first time Mom went to jail before rent was due. I couldn't pay the rent. I was just a kid myself, with two younger siblings I had to care for.

For now, we were still at the house, and from time to time, a friend of my mom's would come by to check on us. This guy friend had been in love with my mom since they were kids. He would take her on errands and give her money from time to time. He would come over with his older brother, Raabi'a, and help us out while the courts decided how much time she was going to get. Come to find out, Raabi'a liked me. He knew my mom had gone to jail. He would start coming over, asking if we needed anything. Me being a kid and all, I didn't really realize what was going on until he starts offering me large amounts of money.

He started off by giving me money to get my hair done. Then asking me, did I want to go to the mall to buy Nikes and clothes to go with my hair? Of course, I did. These were all the things I always dreamed of having as a kid in high school. All my friends had new clothes and shoes, and I wanted to fit in. I wanted to look nice too.

After that, he would start telling me he was going to pick me up from school early so we could go buy clothes and shoes. It got to the point that he would take me to his house after we left the mall. He would act like he's going to fix me something to eat, but then he would show me ten hundred-dollar bills and say it was mine if I let him lick my vagina. I never had seen that much money before. I was so scared. He was so old, big and ugly. I let him do it anyway. I needed the money to take care of me and my sisters. Looking back now, I feel I was raped and used.

He had a son that was a little younger than my sisters. He was still with the baby's mother, if I'm not mistaken. Honestly, I don't know where she was at this point in time. I would never see her around or hear of her; I just remember sometimes, when he and his brother would come by the house for my mom, she would be with them. She must have found out at one point what he had been trying to do to me.

He asked me if I had told her. I let him know I was so embarrassed and ashamed, I never told anyone and I never will. After that, he tried a few more times. He had started wanting to have sex with me and offering more money. I never did anything with him after that first time.

My mom gets out of jail two weeks later. Rent is due. I pay the rent to help her. I don't tell her how I got the money, and she didn't even really care. She was simply happy I gave her $700. A few months later, things started getting bad. My mom couldn't even pay the rent anymore.

We move in with Auntie Jackie and her three kids, Vadimir, Jah and Dee. They lived right by the Encanto 62nd trolley station, not too far from where we were staying on Imperial and 50th Street. Auntie Jackie was a close friend of the family for as long as I could remember. My grandma Stella and her mom were best friends before my grandma died. Auntie Jackie would always tell me stories about how she couldn't stand my dad.

I remember her telling me a story about she and my dad fighting over me when I was a baby. She had come to the house to pick my mom up. She and my dad had an altercation because my dad didn't want me to go. He told Auntie Jackie to take my mom and leave his house. But she refused. She wouldn't go without me too. She had one of my legs and he had one of my arms and they were fighting over me like a crazy game of tug of war.

One of the benefits of us moving to Auntie Jackie's house was that Farrell lived literally five minutes away from her. Plus, he felt comfortable coming to her house. Before, he would say I lived in the "bross town," which was the wrong territory That's why he would never come to my house when I lived on Imperial. Back then, I was so happy he never tried to come to my house; I was mortified at the thought of him seeing how I was living. Now though, he said it's cool. He's comfortable with me living in Encanto. That's his neck of the woods.

It was fun living with Auntie Jackie. It was different. We always had food. She had cable and lots of movies. My cousin Dada would bring her son TJ over. My cousin Vadimir and I would babysit for her while she went to do hair downtown at the hair gallery. My cousin would pay us and hook our hair up when she had extra time. She had lots of clients and made good money, but my little cousin TJ was bad as hell. He would call us "bitches." He was only two years old. She would pay us well because nobody else wanted to watch him.

Farrell's at my house every day, as soon as he gets off work. He would go home, shower, take care of his business, and ride his bike straight to my house. Don't ask me why he would ride his bike He had a car.

Auntie Jackie would be at work and my mom would be wherever, so it was cool. We even had sex again. This second time around, he really does everything. I mean, everything he was supposed to do the first time when he tricked me. It doesn't hurt as much either. After that, I instantly fall in love. I'm thinking to myself, that was worth it.

Lamya spends the night with me at Auntie Jackie's this weekend. She comes to show support and hang out, knowing I don't have my own place anymore. My mom loved Lamya. Lamya was her baby, and Lamya loved my mom.

Mom would never let me go to her house though. Lamya would always have to come to mine. But then one day she was over and Keyna told my mom that she had seen Boo underneath the covers with his head moving, and Lamya's legs were open and she was making noise. After that, my mom said Lamya couldn't come over ever again. Lamya didn't care. I knew it was boring for Lamya when she would come over my house anyway. I wasn't allowed to do anything, and we never had food.

She lived close to Auntie Jackie, but she's never spent the night there so it's something new for all of us. I was missing her anyways, since she stopped going to Lincoln. She had to leave Lincoln to get her grades and credits together so she can graduate on time. It all worked out for the better for her, so I couldn't complain.

Lamya and I have literately known each other our entire lives. We went to Johnson Elementary together, located in Emerald Hills, and she was the first friend I met in kindergarten. At the time, I lived down the hill in these apartments called Bayview Heights. Lamya lived in a house in the Emerald Hills community.

By second grade, we had become best friends. Lamya never judged me, even though she was raised a lot better. She always treated me fair, not like I was poor and needed her charity. Still, I wasn't happy the times she would come to school with two bags of chips and two snacks, but she wouldn't give me my own bag of chips for nothing. I would have to snatch them and run sometimes. Then she got smart. She would start spitting in the bags of chips so I wouldn't snatch them and run.

She would love issuing me out a little at a time, knowing I was hungry.

For the most part, us being friends took away some of my insecurities about my poverty growing up. She was normal to me. And I admired her because she had her dad, who took really good care of her and her sister Maeva and worked for UPS.

I loved her dad, Uncle Tel. Regardless of what he was going through, you couldn't help but respect the man. Lamya and I also had a lot in common. Our birthdays are a day apart, we shared the same middle name, and our first names both start with the letters L and A. That's what we would say to people growing up. That's why we were best friends. She is a lot thicker, cute face, also dark complexion. She was banged out; she was from a gang.

Being Lamya's best friend was probably the reason they thought I was from Emerald Hills. It was crazy! I got in more fights with the Skyline girls than some of the real gang banging girls. I wasn't even a gang member, though Lamya would try and make me one. I was labeled all the same because my friends and family were Bloods.

Lamya knew most of the East Side affiliates from going to Keller Middle School. Keller is located near Skyline, and most of the kids who went to Keller were from Skyline Park. I went to Lewis Middle School, which was located a little way away in San Carlos. Maybe because Lamya went to Keller and she was friends with most of the East Side people, she got a pass. They never would trip on her. I really wasn't introduced to the East Side until I got with Farrell.

Lamya smoked weed and started having sex way before me. She would tell me I needed to hurry up and lose my virginity. The longer I waited, the more it was going to hurt. I needed to get that part out the way. Little did she know, I had a story to tell her.

She always liked hanging around older people when she was young. Don't get her twisted either — she will sex your man. She is not tripping.

She even had sex with Tanu. He mentioned to me that he would tell her how he was still in love with me and she knew in high school how he was. She still had sex with him. She wasn't tripping; I wasn't either. That's my bestie, and you just had to love her. You know the saying: it ain't no fun if the homies can't have none.

Her sister Maeva was way more advanced than most people I knew. I love that girl. I looked up to her like the big sister I never had.

Maeva had braces and wore glasses, but that didn't stop the boys from liking her. She had a nice body for being skinny, unlike me. I was a pole, no titties or booty.

I'll never forget, we were in elementary and Maeva barged into the girl's bathroom, telling everyone, "Move out my way! I'm on my period, I got to change my pad." She said whatever was on her mine.

They both were cool as a fan funny, had great sense of humor and bubbly personalities. Lamya and I have been through a lot together. When I say differences, I don't even know how we made it through some of the stuff.

We're just chilling listening to music. My favorite song is on, "How

Did You Get Here" by Deborah Cox. We're eating popcorn, drinking soda, girl talking and catching up, laughing. Vadimir's with us, until her boyfriend Avaaz comes over. They had been dating for a few years. She leaves the room, which gives me a chance to tell Lamya everything that's been going on with me and Farrell. I didn't know if she still likes him or not. They haven't seen each other in a long time. I must let her know what's up before it's too late or someone else tells her. I want her to hear from me first, otherwise I won't hear the last of it.

I fill her in with the gossip. She doesn't really express any feeling or emotions, but that's just how we get down; we're Sagittarius, after all. I don't know what to think of her reaction though. I let her know he told me about her liking him, how he never liked any of the girls that used to come to his house.

Any girl that came over basically was for anybody. I didn't know if Farrell was lying about not being interested in my friend or what, even though I was trying to give him the benefit of the doubt; you know how dudes are over girls with that good. So, I wanted to hear Lamya's side of things. He said he didn't have sex with any of the girls that liked him. And I really wanted to believe he was a free man when I met him, that everything was good between us. He is my man, and I am the chosen one.

Lamya wasn't tripping. She did tell me that one time, when she went over his house with Taguhi, he tried to have sex with her. I found it hard to believe he only got as far as trying. After all, she had been sexually active for quite some time, so if she really liked him like he said she did, why didn't they do it?

I took both sides into consideration. I'm thinking to Lamya, damn, you can't like everybody! She's talking to another dude, so I can only assume everything's good.

She would always be around a lot of dudes.;. Her house was the hot spot growing up. Anytime you want to see guys, all you do is go to her house. There, you can do whatever. That's why my mom never let me go.

I end up moving in with my cousin Dada after living with Auntie Jackie for a few months. I really don't know how I ended up moving to my cousin's place, but somehow, I ended up there while my two sisters stayed with Auntie Jackie. I think I started getting on Auntie Jackie's nerves. I felt like I started to get picked on after my cousin Jay and his baby momma moved in with their kids, and I started talking back.

I guess I had a smart mouth, is what I was told. But it didn't matter; I had options. The space was getting limited anyway. Dada had start picking me and Vadimir up from school often, and we would do fun stuff together. She was fun, and older, and cool to be around. She wasn't tripping off Farrell either, so I had nothing to worry about. She had met him, she liked him, and would let him come over whenever.

Lamya and Aaliyah would also come over. We all liked it better over at her house, where we had more freedom than I'd ever experienced. She wasn't tripping, Auntie Jackie didn't care, and my mom sure didn't care either. She was too busy ripping and running, doing her.

I remember I threw a pool party shortly after I moved in with Dada. I invited so many people and everyone showed up. It turned out nice. We had music, food, drinks, you name it. I was happy my first pool party was the turn up.

I ain't gone lie — one thing that did irritate me that day was, my homegirl Jaasau pulls up with Farrell and my best guy friend Rana. I always had a crush on him, but we were always just friends. He was the type of boy that was growing up fast. He started trying to pimp at a young age. I knew I never stood a chance with Rana. We were on two different pages. I wasn't tripping either, he was just my eye candy. Farrell had no ideal I felt this way, and I had known him way before meeting Farrell.

I didn't want any of my friends dating him. Farrell was like Jaasau's godbrother, she would say, so he was the least of my concern. But Rana was always fine to me, and I suspected she liked him, or he liked her, or both.

I hated the fact that they pulled up together, period. I didn't say anything, it really wasn't my place, but that's the way I felt. On top of it, Jaasau was cute, with a cute body. I wasn't feeling that.

Rana and Farrell were from the same gang. I guess you can say that Rana was Farrell's younger homie. He was younger than Farrell by just a few years. In my head, I'm thinking to Jaasau, go find someone else to like. I can't remember if she was still dating my cousin Taisito or not at this time. I didn't really care, so long as she left Farrell alone. He was my eye candy. I don't know why I became so overprotective in that situation, but I was.

Around 2000

Shortly after that, my cousin Dada moves out of that house she had been sharing with her mom, taking her three boys and moving in with her boyfriend in Emerald Hills on Bollenbacher. She asked me if I wanted to come with them. She said there was an extra room for me. I really didn't want to go back to Auntie Jackie's house (she had too much going on there) and I had gotten used to living with Dada.

And Dada, she wasn't going to leave me. She was cool with me coming with her to her boyfriend's, so I packed up and went.

I'm not gone lie; I was enjoying the freedom I had living with her. Ever since my sisters were born, there had never been a time when I did not have to take care of them. Finally, I could come and go as I please. Without always having my sisters there, I had so much freedom I didn't know how to act. I straight up felt like I was on vacation! I still had to do babysitting from time to time, and only when I was free, so it didn't feel like I was a mom anymore.

So, when Dada asked if I wanted to go with her, I just asked, "When are moving?"

Without sounding selfish, I was really trying to take full advantage of the situation. I knew I had to go get my sisters eventually. My mom was going to start tripping, trying to be a real mom. It wouldn't be long before she needed help again.

As for my sisters, they liked Auntie Jackie's house. Anything was better than living with just Mom. Not that they didn't love her or miss being in their own place, but they were a lot younger than me, too young to understand what Mom's addiction was doing to us. But me? I didn't miss none of it.

I would pick my sisters up or go hang out with them at Auntie Jackie's house a few times out the week. A part of me felt bad and guilty for leaving them. I knew that's what they were used to, people leaving them, and they didn't know any better. I would always think about them and pray that they weren't mad at me for leaving them too, after my mom had already left them. I just felt I needed a little space, and this was my chance to get it. So, I went with my cousin Dada and tried to make the most of my new life.

It was cool living at her dude's house. We called him Meat. Lamya lived around the corner and I would walk to her house sometimes. The only thing was Farrell, didn't like the fact that I'd moved to Emerald Hills.

Him and the Emerald dudes would feud. They were from revel gangs. He wasn't allowed up there under any circumstances. He would pick me up from school and we would go to his house and chill, but he could never bring me back home. Dada would pick me up from his house when it was time to go.

Eventually, Farrell got tired of ditching and dodging bullets trying to drop me off. So, he bought me my first car. It was a grey hatchback Honda with a stick shift. He tried teaching me how to drive. He took me to the back of O'Farrell Park, showed me the break the gear and how to shift it, what was first, second, third, reverse. I tried, but it wasn't happening. Farrell had no patience whatsoever. By the end, pretty much he told me, this is my car, but if I wanted to be in traffic, I'd have to teach myself.

It literally took me a week to learn how to drive a stick. I'm not saying I was a pro; I knew how to get from point A to point B.

I remember the second day driving to school from Meat's house. It was me and my homegirl Ujarak in the car that day. She grew up with us at Johnson Elementary School and lived with her grandmother in Emerald Hills. She was always one of my good friends and loved me and looked out for me. She would walk to my house to keep me company and ride with me to school.

Our school was up a hill from Meat's house. Hills weren't my favorite. I struggled with them, and I would always try to avoid driving up or down a hill if possible. But there were no avoiding hills this morning we were running late. We are going up the hill, and I don't shift in time. I roll back and bump into a car behind me. All bad! I looked in my rearview mirror and saw I'd just hit the car of a Hispanic lady. I had to ditch her. I had no choice. I had no license no insurance, and I was in deep trouble if I got caught.

I had just gotten my car. I was happy to be driving. Don't get me wrong, from time to time I could get lucky and get the keys to Dada's truck, but that couldn't compare to having your own car. I wasn't about to give that up. I apologized to the woman in my head, then said, "Hold on, Ujarak! We out of here." I got us to school safely, in one piece, by the grace of God. This whole time next to me, Ujarak's busting up laughing! That was my homegirl. She was solid. I love Ujarak.

It is my senior year. Farrell decides he's no longer having the situation with me living at Meat's house in Emerald Hills, car or not. He's just frustrated with the whole thing. He wants me to be around 24/7 so he can see what I'm doing. I'm happy with it. Me and my man finally get to live together. I was tired of leaving him anyway.

I remember moving into his house. It was cold. He didn't have much in the house, as his dad was in the process of selling it. The previous tenants who Farrell had lived with there had moved out.

All he had was a black couch in the den, his twin size bed and a dresser he had moved into the master bedroom with a floor heater. The shower — we called it "the whale" — was just an old, broken-down tub, tarnished and stained. The shower head didn't work, so you had to bathe in a crouching position, crunched over to get under the water. It got the job done, but barely.

We would be freezing in that house. When I say we would cuddle, we really had to cuddle to keep warm. We would really be in there enjoying each other's company, chopping it up. I wouldn't have changed it for the world.

We would go to the neighborhood convention store, on Skyline Drive, to get hot chocolate, a hotlink and chips with some nacho cheese and jalapenos. It was good, plus I love nacho cheese.

Then we would go back to the house to eat, smoke weed, then shower so we could love each other up. That was our daily routine when I came home from school and Farrell got back from work.

I'm living there a little while what I start to get scared, realizing that my period never came this month. I thought it might be from the stress of everything that's going on.

But in the end, I couldn't deny it. I'm pregnant! It was all that cuddling. I can't believe it. Birth control pills failed me. I don't know what to do. I tell Lamya, whom I trusted with this situation because she had been through it before.

I don't know what the hell to do. I go to Planned Parenthood and they tell me I'm going on two months. I let Farrell know I'm pregnant. He's excited, even though he knows how I feel about having kids right now; that's the reason I had gone on birth control. I felt like I already had kids to raise, and I knew my parenting days wasn't over with having to take care of my two sisters. I was just getting a break, and now this. It was the worst timing ever.

Around October 2001

Senior year Homecoming, I'm getting ready and we're both very annoyed. Farrell can't attend Homecoming; he wasn't allowed at any of Lincoln festivities. Anybody affiliated with Morse High wasn't allowed at any Lincoln High event, and both sides knew that if they got together, someone would end up hurt.

I'm confused about being pregnant. I want to be done with Lincoln High, to just fast forward to Prom and get it over with. Besides my man can't come to any dances with me, I'm over it. I just want to move on so I can live my life with Farrell. I'm feeling overwhelmed by all this drama, and my feelings and emotions are everywhere.

I kept it cool. Aaliyah end up being my date. We made the best of it. We looked cute. I remember she had on all black with a waterfall swoop ponytail and I had on all turquoise with a high ponytail. We had gotten our nails and feet done the same color as our outfits. We looked good and we knew it.

It's my senior year. I'm feeling myself and no one could tell me nothing. I'm driving now, I had a different hair style almost every week, and I'm stealing lots of clothes and shoes. I was fitted from head to toe every day.

Stealing had become the norm for me. It went from stealing groceries to clothes, shoes and whatever else I wanted that I couldn't buy for me and my sisters. Even though my sisters were living at Auntie Jackie's, I still did what I had to do for them, because I knew my mom wasn't helping. She was letting them live there, and that was already enough. There were times she needed help. I totally understood and appreciated her for everything she was doing.

Farrell even start dressing better thanks to my habit. I would get him clothes and shoes too. Farrell and I shared a strong bond. No one could come between us — and believe me, they were trying. I loved living with him. I was living my best life ever.

Sometimes, I would bring my homegirl Aaliyah over when I knew Farrell would have his homies over too. Aaliyah started talking to one of his homeboys. She started feeling him. The whole situation was kind of a foul on my part. I knew this guy had a girlfriend name Sabri, a girl I had become good friends with.

Sabri reminded me of Charlie Baltimore. She was one of the Morse High girls who didn't care that I went to Lincoln. She wasn't trying to bang on me, and fight for whatever reason. She acted like a lady.

I had to hook Aaliyah up. My brother Reg was tripping, hoeing all around Lincoln. I think he had even start dating somebody else. There were so many rumors about him, it just broke Aaliyah's little heart.

When I explained to Farrell about how I felt bad for introducing Aaliyah to his friend, he said I shouldn't feel foul about anything since he's the one telling me to bring her over. So, it was all Farrell's doing. I had just been doing what I was told. If I put my girl Aaliyah up, what happened next wasn't my fault. As Farrell said, everybody is for everybody.

I did miss Sa'adha being around. When Farrell and I started getting serious, we found out Jabez was messing with my cousin Faas, the same one he had been seeing from before. Sa'adha had moved on too. She had a new man who went to a different school and she was really liking her new guy. I was okay with that. We still saw each other and she was still my main homegirl, even though me and Aaliyah had grown closer. We were all cool.

This whole time, my mom is still living with Auntie Jackie. I'm still in school, but I'm eighteen now. I'm grown, and I don't have to listen to anyone anymore. I decide that I'm staying right where I'm at, even if Mom does ever get her own place again. She didn't like the fact that I'm living with Farrell but there's nothing she can do about it. Besides, it wasn't like she was taking care of any of her kids. Still, she ends up meeting him.

By now, I didn't care how she felt about anything I was doing. It was all her fault that I'm in my situation.

This wouldn't have happened if she had been at home, caring for us as a real mother. I would have never end up living with a guy, going through half of the stuff I had to go through. Keyna and Trice loved Farrell, and he loved them, and that's all that mattered to me.

Farrell and I are still living in his father's house, still having fun, my cousin Dada starts coming over more, bringing drinks, weed, cooking meals for us. I guess one thing ends up leading to another, and one day the same homeboy that was talking to Aaliyah starts inquiring about my cousin Dada.

This homeboy, everybody wanted him. He was alright. Farrell didn't care if the situation got messy, he just hooked everybody up. He was playing matchmaker for real. He let my cousin Dada know his boy was interested, and from there they went on a few dates. She was totally feeling him, and he was feeling her too. I think he was getting aroused. She was older, probably had lots of experience and stuff to offer, that was something he had never experienced. I felt bad for my friend, but I couldn't do anything about it.

Still, I had to let Aaliyah know what was going down. I am not gone lie, I was feeling very awkward at first about how Dada just walked in and stepped on my homegirls' toes. But Dada wasn't tripping she was hearing that Meat was cheating.

Aaliyah wasn't just any friend. She would spend the night with me, get her hair done by my cousin and everything. I loved this girl. Damn! It was crazy how things just took a turn. I was even mad at Farrell.

I knew Aaliyah should have dated one of my close childhood best friends, instead of the eye candy. My homeboy Jabir, whom I grew up with, was in love with Aaliyah. He was in love with her the way Tanu was in love with me back in the day. Anytime he would be over, he would always ask about her and tell me how much he was in love with her, ask me to call her, go get her, hook them up. He would say beautiful things about how much he adored her. Why is it we never want the ones that are good for us?

Eventually, everything was back to normal. I guess Aaliyah was the type to never express how she really felt, plus she knew my cousin Dada and she loved her too. She really wasn't going to say too much about the situation. It's just a man.

So now it was Farrell and me, Dada and her man. When we were double dating, my cousin damn near moved in. She was there every day with the kids, and Farrell and his homeboy would be babysitting the boys, at times driving her truck. Stuff was getting wild with so many people around. It turned into a straight-up party house; in those days, there wasn't ever a time we weren't turning up.

I eventually confide in my mom about my situation. When she saw me bring food over one day, she asked me was I pregnant. She knew. She wouldn't hear anything I had to say about it. All she said was, "You don't need no kids, Lacole. You need to get an abortion. You already got your sisters you need to take care of." Oh, the stories our bodies would tell if they could talk.

My mom had told me in the past that I would have had about ten brothers or sisters if it weren't for abortion; I knew she had lots in her past. So, it was straight to the abortion clinic I go.

I went to the Planned Parenthood in Mission Valley. I will never forget that visit. I remember coming out hungry because you weren't supposed to eat any food prior to the surgery. I had no food in my stomach for about 24 hours. We went to Wendy's afterward, before we hopped on the freeway. All I can remember is excruciating pain in my abdominal area. The food I tried eating came right up. Farrell had to pull over on the freeway to help me. It was horrible.

Farrell was a little hurt by my decision to get an abortion. He knew we weren't ready for kids, but he told me we could have made ourselves ready. He knew how stressed I was about the conversation I had with my mom. He wanted the baby, but he respected my wishes — or should I say, my mom's wishes. He had resentment towards my mom for that.

In truth, I really wasn't ready for kids. My mom had already embedded in me that's I should not have kids yet, plus I was smoking and drinking, not taking care of my body. Farrell wasn't too happy about it, but in the end, it was my life and my body. Plus, I had just got done raising my sisters; I just couldn't go right back into that. I was just starting to enjoy my life. I'm sorry. I just couldn't do it.

A few months later, Farrell gets a call the house is finally being sold. We have a few weeks to get out.

Things are starting to come to an end. We don't know exactly when someone would be buying the house, we just know it's coming soon. We start turning up every night, more than usual, trying to use the last of our time here.

And then, our time runs out. We must move. I don't know why the whole time his dad was telling him the house will be sold, Farrell wasn't taking it seriously. He made no effort to look for somewhere to live. It got to the point Dada was getting us rooms at hotels until that got too expensive.

Farrell had asked his mom if he could move in with her. I was going to go back to Auntie Jackie's house until we figured it out.

Farrell ended up moving in with his mom, Ms. Tam He didn't like the fact that we were apart again. He tried moving me in with him and his mom. The first night, it worked. She wasn't having it after that. Honestly, I didn't think his mom ever liked me. The way she would talk to me at times and act when I was around was weird. I never disrespected her though.

She probably thought her son deserved better. I could be wrong, but that's the vibe I would get. I loved Farrell so much, I never paid it any mind. I never mentioned it to him that his mom was unwelcoming to me. I wasn't trying to come in between them. I would think, maybe she'll get to know me and think differently one day.

Farrell didn't get it though. "Why is it a problem that she stays here?" he asked his mom. "We'll only be here at night, we'll sleep on the floor,

I'll even give you money. Can she just stay until I find a place? I'm looking right now." He's sounding desperate.

But Ms. Tam was firm. "No, Farrell, she can't stay. I don't want your money. I'm your mother not hers. Where is her family?"

"Why does it matter where her family is? Let's go, Cole," He stomps out, furious. We sleep in the car for the first time, parked in front of his mom's house. It's chilly. I wasn't looking forward to getting used to this. I tell him, "I would rather try and sneak you into Auntie Jackie's house instead of all this."

He didn't want that. I guess it was his pride or he didn't want to risk getting me in trouble. I don't know. Two weeks of that though, and Farrell was fed up. He couldn't take being away from me longer, and under these circumstances we were stuck sleeping in the car. Back and forth, from his mom's house to my auntie's house, we park and sleep just wherever.

Farrell picks me up from school one day, He's so excited, he's damn near in tears. He had found us a place. 8765 Delrose Avenue, in Spring Valley. I'll never forget that address. We go straight there, he gives me my key, looks me in my face and says, "I love you. Won't nobody be taking this away from us unless we don't pay our rent. I got you."

He starts smiling and crying at the same time. I just fall into his arms, hug him so tight and tell him I love him with all my heart and appreciate him so much. I just couldn't believe he got us an apartment.

Farrell picks up a side hustle, starts selling weed. His clientele picked up fast and he is making a pretty good profit. He then bought himself a beat-up Cutlass. He hooked it up, painted it powder blue, put nice 20-inch rims on it and added some loudspeakers. It was clean!

The only problem was, I tried driving it to school a few times and the homies weren't having it. They would press me. They would threaten to mess up his car. That was too much for me. I went back to driving the Honda.

Farrell didn't care about the threats though. He would still tell me to drive it to school with a smile on his face. I really didn't want to take that chance. I didn't want the smoke; I'm good! I really believed he wanted them to try and mess it up so he could have a reason to be up there, acting a fool. That wasn't gone happen on my watch.

He's working, I'm finishing my senior year. I get a part-time job with Dada at the hair gallery downtown, as a shampoo girl. We're doing the damn thing! I am making at least a hundred or more a night.

I am learning how to perm hair, dye hair, and I start really wanting to do hair like my cousin. I'm planning on going to beauty school when I graduate.

Everything is going well. It seems like all that stuff we went through was worth it. It made our bond that much stronger. When we moved into our own apartment, it was like we were inseparable. We were best friends and partners in everything, like Bonnie and Clyde. It felt good to have someone love me that much, and I knew the love was real.

While things were finally good in my life, my mom had gone back to jail for the same thing again. Except this time, they weren't playing with her. They decided to give her three months in Las Colinas, a women's detention facility, and a drug program called Kiva to complete after she was done with her jail time.

When she arrived at Kiva, it was a cool surprise for her that Maeva was there at the program finishing her time. This was the same Maeva I'd known since forever, my girl Lamya's cool older sister. When I would take my sisters to go visit our mom, I would see Maeva and be happy she was doing good.

I made sure my mom was straight. She had gained weight from being sober and she looked nice. I stole her lots of clothes and shoes. She was happy. I'm doing me at this point, not looking back.

When my mom gets out of the program, she needs somewhere to live. She knows Farrell and I have our own spot, from what I'd told her while she was away. I know she feels I'm obligated to let her come live with us, but for some reason she would always use my sisters as a guilt trip. It worked every time. Plus, she really didn't have anywhere else to go. She couldn't go back to my auntie Jackie's house. Before she went to jail, she got kicked out of there for something coming up missing. Once again, I had to sacrifice.

I talked to Farrell about it. The thing about him was, he was down for whatever I wanted. I never heard "no" from him. We were willing to give my mom a chance, since she said she wanted to try and stay clean. She needed support. I feel she deserved a chance. Everybody deserves a chance.

Having her and my sisters staying with us was cool at first, and then my mom relapsed. She had to go at that point. Suddenly, she couldn't stand Farrell. She felt he was the reason she had to leave. She leaves and tries to hurt me by taking my sisters.

They go live at my aunt Daisy's, on Euclid and Oliver. That really hurt me, to see my sisters go with her under these conditions. There wasn't anything I could do about it though. That's my mom. After that, I took a break for a while from the whole situation from being mentally drained, didn't talk to her for a bit. I felt it would be best. Having her in my life was too much stress with her being high. I just knew my sisters was going to have to suffer for it, and that was the only thing killing me inside.

Farrell and I continue doing us. We enjoyed our apartment alone. I had to focus, as it was getting closer to graduation. When Grad Night is over, I'm happy. Again, Farrell couldn't come, same drama, different day.

Then, it's time to start looking for prom dresses. The whole process is depressing, knowing Farrell is not coming with me. I was tired of going to these dances with my friends. Me and my homegirl Sheen made the best of it. It was bad for her also. Her dude was in jail our senior year, so like me, she had no date.

We decided to be each other's date. We were going to the dance in style. We took our play daughters Dakila and Taguhi to Horton Plaza downtown and, with their help, stole Jessica McClintock dresses that were ticketed somewhere around $400. Mine was orange and hers was dark pink. We had even snatched gloves to match.

Around June 2001

The morning of the dance, I went to Hair Ballers and got what they called a cluster. It was an up-do, a French manicure and a pedicure. I was on point. All that was left was to make sure I had some weed, and then I was ready to go.

Sheen looked pretty. She drove her cousin's burgundy Lexus. We had us a bottle of Alize and went to the prom. After the dance was over, we tried going to the hotel afterparty, but after thirty minutes, Farrell realizes prom should be over and he starts calling, wanting me to come home. No partying for me.

I get home, and I'm livid. I scream at Farrell, "Just because you are not able to attend anything, don't spoil my memories of my life!" You're only a senior once. When he was my age, he got to experience his senior activities with his girl. I really felt like this moment was being taking away from me.

But it is what it is. I knew what I was dealing with. I really wish he could have come. I really was missing him not being able to be at any of my senior activities. Senior year is incredibly special to a girl. This is the love of my life. I wanted to make these memories with him.

Shortly after that, it's graduation day. I'm pumped up! It's finally about to be over. All I can remember is me Sheen and Aaliyah in our white cap and gowns with our white dresses underneath on the bus riding downtown happy we bout to graduate taking pictures on our polaroid cameras.

Farrell gets ran out of my graduation by the Lincoln Park Bloods. He tells me when I make it home that he got to see me walk across the stage, but from there, it was a wrap. He said the wrong crowd spotted him. He had to run for his life. I'm just thankful that he made it home to tell the story. I can't tell you what Farrell was doing in those streets when I wasn't around. He only told me what he wanted me to know. Even so, I knew that having to run for your life means it's serious.

Another thing that sucked about him getting ran out my graduation was, my dad had just made it home from prison after serving a ten-year sentence. He got to make it to my graduation. I was thrilled! Seeing him there really surprised me. I didn't know exactly when he was getting released. I really wanted Farrell to meet him as soon as possible. I was so happy he was home. We had catching up to do. I was my dad's only child.

While my dad was in prison, I would write my dad letters and tell him all about Farrell. He knew I was pregnant. He knew I had gotten an abortion. He was upset my mom had told me to kill the baby.

That's what happens when you leave your daughter and go to prison. You really can't blame anybody but yourself. The relationship between me and my dad was strange: even though he wasn't there like he should have been, he was still my favorite parent.

I always remember the good times from when he was there. I remember him bringing me a big Easter basket to school with cupcakes for me and all my friends. He had just got out of jail for the first time back then. He would tell me stories about when I was younger, how him and my mom would always tell jokes and clown people.

One day we were leaving 7-Eleven, and my parents were talking, forgetting I wasn't strapped into my car seat. My dad makes a fast stop at the light and I went sliding underneath the seat. Slurpee flew everywhere. What's when they realized I hadn't been strapped in! My dad said I never cried as a kid, even when I got hurt.

My mom hated the fact I loved my dad so much. She would call him a no-good buster and would say he ain't shit and that he never did shit for me. But I love his dirty dross. I would think to myself, what's the difference?

Around June 2001

My mom didn't do nothing either but bully me. We just lived together. What makes that any better?

If I had to say what made my relationship with my dad so special, I would chalk it up with my dad being alright with almost anything. He was good at keeping things a secret. He did what he had to do when he was around. I was comfortable with being open with him, and he never laid a finger on me. Our bond stayed close, even though he was doing time. He was way nicer to me than my mom ever was. I really didn't understand why she was so hard on him.

My sisters' dad, in the other hand, Mom loved him to death. I would see him whoop her butt. He even attacked me for trying to help her once. He was never a good provider for our family. I've never even seen the Negro work before. To me, it was like he was a big kid — he needed everything taken care of for him. Maybe I was too young to understand, but I didn't know what she saw in him.

I just knew, if I ever have kids, no one would be putting their hands on my children. One day, I pull up to see him hitting my mom in the face. I get out the car, push him back yelling at him to stop, then go to pick my mom up off the ground.

While I'm bent over helping my mom, he kicks the mess out of me from the back, aiming right in my private part. It was the worst pain I've ever felt. I must have fallen to the ground.

I was numb for a minute. When I managed to collect my thoughts, I got my mom and got the hell up out of there. I wasn't about to try and fight this man. He's really fighting back. My mom always had bad taste in men.

While my dad was in prison, he got married to a lady name Maayan. She was from China. She didn't know English. My dad met her online when he was in prison. My dad helped her get citizenship to come to the U.S. They lived in an apartment in East Diego. She was a genuinely nice lady from what I knew of her. I loved her as my stepmom.

I don't think my dad was truly in love with her. I know that he didn't stay faithful to her for long. She would call my phone looking for him, barely speaking enough English to tell me she hasn't seen him in days. I

Healed

wouldn't know what to tell her. I felt bad for her and wished my dad would do her right.

Come to find out, he was cheating and in a relationship with a whole 'another woman. He had my little brother with her a few years later. You wouldn't believe who the woman was. When I found out, I was shocked! I couldn't even stomach it. It got to the point that it was hard for me to even go around the situation. I really didn't even see my brother much when he was born.

I really think my dad was foul for dating Deana. She was my mom's youngest brother Vernus's wife. My uncle died shortly after that. I remember him telling me before he died that he was hurt; he couldn't believe my dad had done that to him. He had other health complications, but I think he died of a heartache. I felt his pain. I loved my uncle Vernus and I was sad for him.

It took talking to Farrell to make me realize things didn't have to be that bad. After all, the situation wasn't my little brother's fault. Eventually, I came around, and it was a joy to be around my brother. He was the handsomest, happiest baby ever, always smiling. I was happy for my dad. He had finally gotten the son he had always wanted.

Farrell loved my brother. He was happy to see me be a part of my dad's life. He knew how important that was to my dad, whom he loved. He always said, my dad can bake dessert good. He would go over there, high with the munchies, always asking him to bake something. My dad would love Farrell's company so much he would do it.

Farrell had a nickname for my dad, Jamie. My dad loved it. He would be cracking up! That was cute to me. I was glad Farrell and my dad got along so well. They were the most two important men in my life.

I later come to find out about a girl who was having sex with Farrell back in the day before I came around. Sure, we all have a past, but turns out this girl has a daughter — allegedly Farrell's child. This is my first-time hearing any of this. Can you say shell shocked? My world is turned upside down. What is going on?

Farrell is telling me about this girl he supposedly has a baby with. Why am I just hearing this stuff like this?

I'm sitting on the bed, rubbing my forehead in disbelief. If he thinks he can spring this on me, he has it coming. "You mean to tell me, I got an abortion, now the next female saying she has your child? You got me twisted!" Even though the reason for my abortion was that I didn't want kids, still, I didn't want anyone else having kids by him. I was the girl. Period.

Farrell's nearly as angry as I am. He says, "Man, I don't have no kids! This girl is starting to say I'm her baby daddy after she found out the dude she was blaming before, it ain't his."

"Well, why is your name in the mix? Were you really having sex with her?" I ask.

"Yeah, me and all the rest of the homies. I wasn't the only one smashing blood on the set."

"Well, personally, I'm not worried about the homies, Farrell I'm not in a relationship with the homies. When was this and how along ago? Everything else is irrelevant."

"Way before you, Cole." "How long before me?"

"I don't know, before you! That ain't my baby."

I'm skeptical. How can this sort of thing not be something you keep track of? I say to him, "I hope this information isn't true, Farrell. I think this is something you really should have told me about if you had any doubts."

"Don't worry about it, it's not. These hoes be hating. They want what you got, Cole. I am not paying none of them hoes any attention and that's the problem. These hoes buy weed, that's it."

Farrell's words still didn't put my worries to rest, but there was nothing more either of us could say. He loved me, I loved him, and we wouldn't let this come between us.

In the mix of all this, Lamya gave birth to her son, my godson Butter. He was just months older than my brother James. It was cool they both would have each other to play with when I would babysit them both.

My godson was the cutest thing. I nicknamed him Butter when he was born, because he was yellow like a stick of butter. Everyone would think he was my child for that reason, and me and Farrell would pretend that was really our son we played house with Butter. He practically lived with us when he was a baby. My mom would keep his hair braided cute. He didn't want for anything while in our care.

Meanwhile, I got a new job at Pacific Theaters. It was cool, for what it was worth. I worked at Pacific Theaters for about six months, got a new car, a blue Chevy Cavalier four-door with black tint. I wish I could tell you what I did at the job to be able to afford that car. Then, I moved on. I had no choice; I was doing bad things at that job to get more money fast.

Meanwhile, Farrell got a new job working for the urban core downtown.

Around 2002

Farrell told me about this job his friend was working at that I might like. I started working at Say San Diego, a six-to-six program for kids who needed caring for before and after school while their parents were at work. I told all my homegirls about it. Soon, we were all working there.

I didn't like the fact that it was an extended day. I would go to work from 6:00 am to 9:00 am. Then, I'd leave and come back at 1:00 pm and get off at 6:00 pm. It added up to a full eight hours, but the money wasn't quite enough so I picked up a few hours with my cousin again back at the salon.

Farrell's working at the urban core still. He was still selling weed on the side. It's bringing in extra money, enough that he bought a new toy, a Caprice Classic. Farrell's passion was buying cars at the auctions to fix them up and sell them. He would call them his toys.

He got my dad into flipping cars. My dad and Farrell had become so tight. It got to the point that he even took Farrell's side over mine sometimes. When Farrell and I would get in a fight, I would leave and go to my dad's house to spend the night. My dad would call Farrell, and let him know I was there, and tell him he better hurry and come get me, because I can't stay for long. I couldn't believe my own dad got Farrell's back over mine!

A few months pass and the situation about the baby doesn't fade away. I had given it a minute to try and see if the supposedly rumor would die down, but it hasn't. By now, I'm thinking to myself, there must be some truth to this if the word is still spreading like a wildfire.

At this point, I needed to find out what the hell was going on. Clearly, I had to let go of my feelings. I was in denial about the situation, like denying it would make the kid go away. If it is true, everything happened before I even came along. There's not much I can really do now but accept it. I told myself I would try because I was in love. I knew the lifestyle everyone was living, but I had something better.

I felt like this girl still wanted Farrell. I'm trying my hardest not to take this jealousy out on my relationship. Unfortunately, things got worse. For some reason, we decide to go to her house the next day. Her mom opens the door and calls back to her dad. Her dad comes to the door and asks us, "What's up? Who are y'all?"

Farrell starts explaining the situation to the dad. He says, "Your daughter is saying I'm the father of her child.

I want to get to the bottom of this. This is interfering with my household."

By now the girl had come to the door too. Her dad looks at his daughter and says, "I thought the other guy was the father."

She starts babbling nervously, probably feeling embarrassed her dad had said that. The whole time, her dad didn't know what the hell was going on. All he knew was that he had custody of the child. He was caring for the child, and that was all that matters. He didn't care who the dad was. In my eyes, it seemed like he was taking place of the dad.

The situation starts to get ugly. The girl is talking mess to me, saying all sorts of crazy things right to my face. I didn't know how to react. I never was the type to argue back and forth. I think I probably had too much built up frustration from growing up, but I was always ready to fight. We can talk after we fight. She was bigger than me that didn't mean nothing; the bigger you are the harder you fall. May the best woman win!

I'm trying to get to the bottom of this. Farrell is my man!

We're arguing back and forth, and it almost gets to fighting, until her dad steps in and tells us to stop. He was over it, Understandably, he didn't want me arguing with his daughter in front of his house. And I'm never disrespectful to anyone's parents, so we hurry and leave. I'm on fire.

I feel like if I were to see her anytime soon, it will go down. We still didn't get to the bottom of the matter. We still don't know if Farrell is the father or not, no DNA test set up or anything. Through this whole thing, I felt like Farrell didn't even care to find out. He didn't want the responsibility, or for the issue to come between us. I feel the girl's dad made him feel comfortable by saying he had custody and was taking care of the child. Hearing that let Farrell feel he didn't have to man up and get to the bottom of this very irritating situation.

The unresolved issue left lots of tension between us. It got frustrating, and me and Farrell started arguing more than usual. After the girl saw him again, she's really pushing a hard line to try to find out if he's the father or not. She's feeling Farrell for sure. I bet she would have done anything to have him. But for whatever reason, he doesn't want to cooperate with her. He felt deep down inside that there was a possibility the child could be his, and he just didn't want to deal with that.

The baby girl really looked like she could have been Farrell's child. She looked just like Farrell's sister to me. Looking back on it now, I don't know why girls in situations like this can't get along to try and work things out for the child's sake. There was a lot of tension between me and this girl, and I'm not proud of that. I wish I had been mature enough to handle the situation like a lady. But I didn't get it back then. I just believed whatever Farrell was telling me. I shouldn't have taken out my frustrations on the baby's mom, period. She was just a kid herself having a child. These men were taking advantage of her youth. She didn't know no better.

What was crazy was, I had fought her homegirl on Springford in Skyline not to long before that. She had been trying to fight my little cousin Taguhi at Skyline Park for whatever reason, I guess over gang banging stuff.

I wasn't any of their favorites at the time. Anytime they saw me in the street, if looks could kill I'd be one dead girl. I didn't care either. I ain't no punk.

They knew Taguhi, knew she had been labelled as a Lincoln Park girl. She grew up on that side and she had dated Lincoln homies in the past, stayed tossing it up. Her and her best friend Dakila stayed active on those Skyline streets, making it known she was Lempi's girl.

And Dakila, who was one of Taguhi's best friends, had no points to prove. She was dating one of Farrell's little homies and just had Taguhi's back.

Lempi was Farrell's little homie too. He loved Farrell. Whatever Farrell did, he wanted to do too. We called him our son. He was highly active in them streets, but obviously nothing scared Taguhi or no one, because it was whatever, whenever. Honestly, their daughter might have been conceived on our living room floor; that's how close we were.

I remember Auntie Kamal, Taguhi's mom, had moved into a house on Timely in Skyline. She bought a cute green Chevy Tahoe and would let Taguhi drive it from time to time. We would be rolling all through Skyline's streets, looking for Farrell and Lempi.

All this while, things are still boiling with me getting into that fight with the O'Farrell girl who had tried fighting Taguhi. They were mad she didn't beat me up liked planned.

Then, on top of that, me going to this girl's house with Farrell to confront her about the situation with the baby. If they all could jump me, they probably would, but I'm Farrell's girl so they could only do so much.

I'm trying to keep my cool and focus on my relationship with Farrell. Things are messed up! It hasn't been the same since the drama started, and I want everything to be right with us again. I love my man.

Mean time between time, I started talking to my mom again. I had missed her, and I really missed my sisters. I had gotten them a bunch of stuff from Old Navy for Christmas that I wanted to give it to them, so Farrell and I pay a visit to my aunt Daisy's house.

My sisters were so surprised to see us, they ran right into our arms. That just melted my heart. They were excited about all the clothes. I'd gotten them nice jackets, toys, everything. When I say I stole the whole Old Navy store, it was damn close. I just had to make my sisters happy.

They were already going through so much, and I knew they hadn't had anything new in a while since I had stopped coming around.

My mom had fallen back into her addiction again, and badly. I think being at Aunt Daisy's really stressed her out. She didn't have her own place. I was grown and had moved on, and I didn't have time for any more of her drama. I didn't know what it really was. I just know, she's looking bad.

My mom always admired my strength. She once told me I was a strong girl and if anything is ever wrong with me, you wouldn't be able to tell. She said I never show it. I handle it well, and I was wondering if that's why she would put so many responsibilities on me as a child.

I couldn't take seeing her and my sisters living in those conditions. Things in that house were not good. I took my sisters shortly after that, back with me and Farrell.

Then Mom checks herself into a mental hospital. It's her doing her again, and this time I don't know if she was trying to get pills or help. She was sad, depressed, feeling sorry for herself.

I'm happy now, knowing that my sisters are okay. They are my main concern. All I can do is wish the best for my mom, hope and pray she snaps out of whatever it is that she is going through.

My mom shared a lot with me about her past growing up, how she's always had to take care of her four brothers. Whenever she talked about it, she basically made it sound like it was all bad. She never got to enjoy her life. I think her upbringing played a big part in why my mom turned to addiction: she was just doing what she saw, repeating the cycle of her own mother.

I felt like that was also the reason she felt I was obligated to do what I was doing. Her favorite saying was what doesn't kill us only makes us stronger. God doesn't put more on us than we can bare.

I would hate to hear those words. They made me feel like she was trying to find excuses for how she treated me.

Today, I live by those words. I understand now what she was talking about and what it really means to grow through hardship.

I would try and take what my mom had been through into consideration.

I mean, I could not imagine finding my mother on the couch dead. But that's something she had to experience. Honestly, it made me want to be better than that. I couldn't turn out the same way.

I would never take my kids through what I've been through. She would say, I'm the kid, she's the mom. And I'd think, okay, well then act like it. I've been grown for a long time. Please mom, I would plead with her, get yourself together for Keyna and Trice and stop making excuses.

My sisters were still living with me and Farrell at the time. My schedule changed with them in the house. I'm waking up an hour earlier than usual. I have to drive my sisters to O' Farrell Middle School. It wasn't walking distance, but it wasn't far. It was about ten minutes' drive from where we lived. I would drop them off and go straight to work. Farrell would pick them up sometimes, or they would walk to Auntie Jackie's after school, which was down the hill. I would go pick them up from there when I got done handling my business.

The alleged baby mama is hot. Things are not going her way. I really don't know what her intentions were. Somehow, we were on the phone arguing one day and that didn't turn out good! We ended up fighting. She came to the alleyway of my apartment complex with her auntie, this white man, and one of her homegirls. All I can say is, I know she wish she hadn't come.

They pumped her up to get beat up. Luckily, I had my bestie Lamya and my homegirl Aaliyah, and Deana with me, in case things got ugly.

Farrell happened not to be there. It was crazy. Farrell's friend Carlos saw the whole thing from his kitchen window and he called Farrell to let him know I was in the alley whooping butt. Farrell was happy to hear that it wasn't the other way around.

The next day, Carlos brought me the biggest Heineken I've ever seen. Telling me I'm the champion and how well I can fight.

Beating her up didn't solve anything though. Shortly after, we moved. I didn't trust none of them girls. I didn't like the fact that they knew where I lived. I wasn't about to stay living here, knowing they were able to pull up anytime and jump me.

We start looking for a two-bedroom apartment to have space for my sisters. We didn't know how we were going to come up with the extra rent money every month, but we would try. I found a spot down the street from our current apartment, in the Spring Villas right across the street from Rally's on Jamaica.

On top of all that, my mom just left the hospital and needs somewhere to stay again. She's asking for forgiveness. She claims she's tired of the life she was living and finally ready to stop this time. My dumb self-gave her the benefit of the doubt. I let her come live with us once again.

I really wanted the best for my mom, really believed in her. I'd be lying if I didn't say, I was also thinking about the check she gets once a month that could help pay our rent.

Mom surprised me. She stayed clean longer than I expected. She even starts helping with the girls. She would get them up for school, fix them breakfast, help get them ready for the day. I was so proud.

Around February 2002

My dad surprised me around this time and bought me a brand-new PT Cruiser. I wasn't happy at first. I thought PT Cruisers was for older people. I wanted a Chrysler 300. I was very ungrateful.

I made the best of it though. The car was electric blue. Farrell took it, he put 18-inch chrome rims on it and added a loudspeaker so you would be able to hear me coming from down the street. I had the best PT Cruiser in southeast. I would get so many complements from older people.

You would see me coming, bumping Mac Dre, disturbing the peace. I was really the only younger person around with a PT Cruiser, and in the end that was the part that made it cool. I couldn't complain.

I knew my dad was trying to come home and make up for lost times. I knew he felt bad about the last sentence he served and being away from me for so many years. I really enjoyed the stories we shared and the time we spent together when we got the chance.

I had to fill him in on things in my family that had been going on. This was the longest my mom had ever stayed clean. That is, until five months later, when she relapses again. I don't know what made her relapse. When she does, I'm over it. She's getting smart, arguing with me, telling me "Fuck you" and how she doesn't need me.

I tell her, "I'm tired of it all. You keep playing with my feelings and emotions, taking advantage of me. You don't have your part of the rent. You keep lying, telling me how you have the money, but you don't."

In the end, the strain and stress of having her around got to be too much. "Mom, you got to go. Period. I can do bad by myself. I'm done!"

She pulls a magic trick out the box. She had an apartment by the next month when it was time for her to go. She found a little duplex on Churhward. It was just enough room for her and my sisters. She made it work. I was cool with it, knowing my sisters didn't have to go live at another random house once again.

My mom didn't live there for long before she moved her cousin Sue in across the hall from her. The company was good for her. Sue had a car and would take her on her errands, look out for her and my sisters. I was appreciative of all that Sue did. She saved me time and gas.

Keyna and Trice were lucky to finally have their own room. My mom had given them the room, and she would sleep on the couch. I knew they were getting tired of sharing rooms with my mom. They had even experienced living in a shelter, cramped in with her and who knows how many others. They were getting older they needed their own space. They already had to share rooms with each other. I felt bad for my sisters. They have been through a lot.

Meanwhile, Farrell and I are looking for somewhere to move now that my mom and sisters are gone. One of Farrell's homeboys ended up breaking in our bedroom window to steal weed, so Farrell didn't trust living there any longer.

We couldn't find anything right away. We are doing us, partying like rock stars. Farrell is selling more weed then normal. I don't know how his clientele picked up so fast, or how he was making so much more money.

It got to the point that he would take our godson, Butter, fill his diaper up with weed and use him as a decoy. It did get annoying. Girls would be calling his phone late at night just for a $10 sack. I thought it was more to see him, honestly.

Around 2003 & 2004

Eventually, I find out how all this extra money is coming in. Farrell thinks he's slick. He's hanging out with some homies, trying to be a pimp! He's got girls giving him money. I flip out. I could kill this Negro with my bear hands.

When Farrell comes home that day, I tear into him. "I'm disgusted with you! You are out sneaking and lying! I don't want to hear nothing but the truth at this point. You definitely owe me an explanation."

Farrell starts pleading his case. I'm not feeling it at all. He says we need the extra money since we still live in the two-bedroom apartment even though my mom and sisters had moved out. He's telling me I'm the reason we need more money.

He tries to tell me it's not so bad. He doesn't have to do anything sexually with these girls. They just give him money for his protection, really.

"What does that supposed to mean?" I demand. "You mean to tell me, these girls know that you have a woman living with you, a woman you're taking care of, and they're okay with you out with them for a few hours? Why would they sell themselves and then just give you, their money?"

He tried to say, yes, exactly, that's all it is.

I'm thinking, yeah, right. Sure, he was protecting them. He just didn't want me to know what they do when I'm not around so the money wouldn't stop. But I know what's going on. They give him money because they like him, and he's got them thinking he's, their dude. I wasn't born yesterday.

If I were a prostitute, I'd protect myself, keep my own money, do everything for myself. I don't need anyone else managing my money. On top of that, the money these girls make isn't enough to even manage. A few hundred, maybe. Come on. By the time you get gas and something to eat, that money is gone. All that time, just for that.

What's the point if most of the time, the pimp who's looking after you is turning tricks off the money you made for them, taking care of some other woman who's not a prostitute, sleeping with her for free while wining and dining her.

Nope. I'm not buying it. I tell Farrell, "I feel like you're trying to play me, like I'm some naive girl. If that's the case, why are you sneaking? Why didn't you tell me this from the beginning, Farrell?"

I decide to throw him one more chance to make this right. "Let me know what's up. Let me meet her.

Let me ask some questions, since you saying this is what it is."

Farrell agrees. Turns out, I know the girl! I can't believe it. I knew she had been getting down for one of Farrell's homeboys in the past. From my understanding, I thought she worked at the urban core now.

I'm thinking to myself, you're Farrell's homeboy's baby mama. Your kid is Farrell and my godchild. Both of y'all scandalous. I couldn't believe what these girls would do for attention, from these dudes and my man at that. They were trained. I wouldn't know if he was having sex with her or not when I'm not around, and that to me was plain gross.

This is stressing me the hell out. I start smoking so much weed, I would get sick. Later, I find out I was pregnant again. The timing this time is no better. I was confused. I didn't even want to tell Farrell about the pregnancy; we were having so many problems. I didn't even know if I still wanted to be with him.

I pack my things and go to my dads' house. Farrell's calling me, begging me to come back home. He tells me he knows he was wrong.

He tells me he's done with everything. He wants to get things back right with me.

It didn't make it any better that my dad took Farrell's side, saying crazy stuff like what he was doing was okay, that it was good if he was taking care of me. He said I had nothing to worry about, that Farrell loves me. If that's the case, then why is he doing this to me?

I'm thinking to myself, Dad, whose side are you on? He should have my back regardless. I stay gone for about a week.

I go back home, but I'm still having doubt and trust issues. I can't believe how Farrell started doing what he was doing. The whole thing wasn't sitting well with me at all. I guess if I'm willing to give him a second chance, I had to move on and let the past be the past. He was good for a second chance.

Farrell really was trying to make up for what he had done wrong. It's working. We're going to Rosario, getting suites, riding horses, eating lobsters, drinking margaritas on the beach, going to E-40 and Kelis concerts… you name it. We're having a blast.

During this period, Farrell picked up an addiction. His choice was Codeine and Promethazine, the same pills my mom would take, but liquid. The drug was nicknamed "lean," and you would really be leaning if you didn't stay active with another drug that's an upper. It was for pain and cough. We weren't experiencing any of that. We would go to 7-Eleven and get a cup of ice, a fruit punch, and sour skittles, mix all of it together and pour the cough syrup inside and shake it around. Of course, I did whatever he did.

I get an abortion around this time too. I go downtown for it. I was feeling bad about even thinking about another abortion, but we were having so much fun. I wasn't ready to give that up yet. I was still young. I'm drinking so much Hennessey, doing lean, smoking weed, I didn't even feel my baby was healthy at that point.

This pregnancy was way worse than the first one. I had so much morning sickness. There was no telling what I was doing to my baby with all the drugs and alcohol. It was a shame. I wasn't too far along, about two months, but I'm not thinking about having a baby. All I wanted was to follow behind Farrell every chance I got. Meanwhile, Farrell really wanted me to have the baby. He said he was ready for a kid.

I told him, "I don't see how, Farrell, when you still need to find out if that little girl is yours our not." I didn't tell my parents about my pregnancy this time. I was ashamed. For sure my mom wasn't going to support me like always, and my dad would have told me to have it. He was ready for a grand baby. He would tell me I was getting old, and that he wanted me to name my baby after him if it's a boy.

I don't listen to any of them. I get the abortion.

Everything is good for about six months. Until one day, Farrell feels our money situation is funny. His car game wasn't really moving how he wanted it to. I didn't know the weed wasn't making enough extra money either. He sold enough of it, plus still working at the urban core. He had become a crew leader, which was like a supervisor, and the promotion had come with a raise. I never wanted much, plus I had a job too. Farrell never made me pay any bills. Besides the costs of my car, he was holding all the weight.

He gets antsy. This time, he's telling me a random girl who buys weed from him wants to hoe for him suddenly. He's probably been having sex with her too. I really have no choice but to let him do what he's gone do unless I wanted to leave him. I stay.

I knew it was wrong. But it's not like I was doing anything to get us any extra money. I just worked at my nine-to-five.

I met this girl. I already know what it is, so I don't even ask her any questions. It's whatever by this point. Farrell starts going back and forth to Anaheim Vegas, getting money.

Me and Farrell did fight over lots of frustration. When we fought, he never put marks or bruises or anything visible on me. He would grab the pressure points on my shoulders and squeeze them so hard I would get weak and fall to the floor. I don't know why that was so painful to me, but it was. When I got up and got my strength back, I would attack him again and he would just grab me and pin me down. I couldn't do anything. He was strong for a guy his size.

While Farrell was out, I would stay home and kick it with Farrell's cousin Sade who had gone to Lincoln with me. She smoked weed and we loved eating, so we would cook together.

Through all that, we just continued working and holding it down. I would sell Farrell's weed to his clients from time to time when I had the time and if I felt comfortable to sell to them.

I started to be okay with the pimping and hoeing too, like it was the normal. I had start thinking I was a madam myself. I would go to National City, which was the track back in the day where the hoes would stroll.

The hoe stroll had lots of women you can choose from of all different races, sizes, you name it. I would act like a top-notch hoe to try and get girls for Farrell. I would dress in all designer clothes. I always had a nice car. I would sell them a dream, like I see the pimps do. The dream is never going to come true for them, you just make them believe it and continue collecting all their money and try and get girls to stay with you. Now that the money is good, you don't want the next pimp trying to come steal yo 'girl.

It worked a few times; I was shocked every time it did. One time, I met a white girl named Snow. She wasn't that attractive to me. I would have preferred something more like a Malibu Barbie type of look. You can tell she really didn't know how to get it, because she really didn't make good money for being white. They would say white girls was the way to go. They made the most money. I didn't know what to do with her when I approached her about being her madam. I was just trying my luck, doing what I had seen others do.

That lasted for about a few weeks, until Farrell came back in town. Then the program changed. She didn't care for Farrell, and he didn't care for her. Farrell said she looked like a smoker. She said if it was just me, she would have stayed, but she had to go. She kept it pushing. It was fun while it lasted.

Around 2005

Farrell's wealth and status starts going on arise, and more money than usual was coming in. You know the saying: more money, more problems. We're upgrading to a bigger place, and big partying. Farrell had found this doctor name Dr. Bowie in east San Diego, where everybody was going to get the Codeine with Promethazine syrup. All you had to do was go in there and act like you have a cough and your chest hurt. This doctor would feel your chest, have you cough, and write you a prescription.

Farrell was paying everybody he knew to go to the doctor. It was $30 a visit. He starts getting bottles. He would sell most of it to make his money back and drink the rest himself. One of his homeboys Davis, who introduce him to the plug, got mad. He felt Farrell was stepping on his toes. He was a heavy user himself, so he would be always thirsty for it. Farrell was the only one that had it at times.

Farrell is addicted to the syrup bad now. He needs it every day, and he doesn't care what anyone else is going through. Mind you, his hustle had been seeing some major improvements. Farrell was no longer working at his regular job once he got that last prostitute. He would say he was an entrepreneur. He sells cars, weed, ass, and whatever else that's moving.

For being young still, Farrell acted much older. I think that's why I was attracted to him. Guys my age were so immature. And I felt like I was already ten steps ahead of most people my age, because I was already raising kids as a child.

We were partying hard, taking Ecstasy pills. Ecstasy took me on another level. When I say I'm ten times hotter than normal, I couldn't stay away from the mirror. I'm the hottest around. Don't let there be a mirror in sight, or I'm in trouble.

When I get my fix, can you say Terminator? It turned me into a feisty little thing. You better not let anyone look at me or my man the wrong way. I remember we were in Tijuana one night, and Farrell got attacked by the security. I just knew we were dead, trying to party hard. When one of us fights, both of us fight. That is just how it went. You can't tell me nothing to calm me down. Them drugs are real. I thank God, we made it home must nights.

Farrell gets the car he's always wanted, a black 1897 Monte Carlo SS. He loves it. It's his pride and joy. All he can think about is fixing it up nice. It didn't look bad when he bought it, just the inside was beat up and it needed a paint job. He didn't have much to really do to it except add on and fix the interior. I was happy for him. He looked nice in it.

We had finally found the time and place to move too. We moved down the street and around the corner to a place on Birch Street. It was in a small complex, a two-bedroom apartment with a washer and dryer in the unit. That was my favorite part of the place. No more laundry room for me. I also liked the fact that it was just me and Farrell. The space was lovely, and we turned the second bedroom into an office.

I'm thinking now, my stuff doesn't stink. I wanted for nothing. I have everything I want and need, and then some. Now that I'm well off, I got so many haters. Everybody wants to fight and I'm not turning down no fades. I'm not scared of no one.

Farrell and I go to this club in Chula Vista for my birthday weekend. I'm all that and some! I have on an all-black and gold Rocawear outfit with some boots to match. They were Jay Z brand, which was poplar back then. My hair is in a black and gold weave. I'm popping, you couldn't tell me nothing.

The minute we walk in, a hater walks up, looking dusty like always. She says, "What's up?" In my head I'm thinking, girl, what you mean "what's up"? She tells me to step outside with her. I tell the hater to take off. I just want to get this over with.

I always spoke the truth. I feel the truth will set you free, but sometimes people can't handle the truth. They get upset and want to fight. I'm fine with that. The truth is going to come out anyway; what's done in the dark always comes to light. Just know, if you put your hands on me, make sure you try and kill me; I didn't take that lightly.

I was always in defense mode. I can fight. I might be only 115 pounds but looks can be deceiving. I'm strong. I dare you to touch me. Girls tried taking advantage of my size. What they didn't realize is, that was one thing I took advantage of too. Being small, I move fast.

This girl accuses me of doing something she didn't like when I was with one of my homegirls from Emerald Hills. They're not here now, so basically, she says, let's fight. I didn't have a clue what she was talking about. I remember laughing and thinking in my head, leave me alone, you high off drugs messing with me. The Emerald Hills girl she was referring to is my best friend Lamya, and the two of them are cool.

I'm mad, shaking my head. It is what it is. I had already fought two girls out of her crew, so I don't know who was going to want to fight me next.

I get up and walk outside with her. Farrell was talking to his homeboy when she and I approached. I kind of feel like it was a setup. I think he distracted Farrell's attention so he wouldn't see any of this go down. Anyhow, this girl and I walk around the corner and start fighting.

This girl immediately starts by pulling my hair. I'm livid my hair is messed up but its typical girl fighting, until she scratches my face by my right eye with something sharp, I think a razor blade. It cut deep. I had a wound on the side of my face for a long time. After that, I'm over it. Either fight fair, from the shoulders, or I don't want to fight. I don't got time for pulling hair and scratching. I'm good at what I do. I was greatly confident and down for whatever came my way. But this took me by surprise they were really trying to mess my face up.

Healed

I never would be the one to call my homegirls and round them up to fight. I didn't have homegirls like that. My best friend Lamya was friends with everybody that didn't like me. That's crazy now that I think about it. If no one else had my back, Farrell did. He didn't care about right or wrong, he had my side through whatever.

After this went down, this girl's brother called Farrell asking what was up with me and his sister. What happen between us? Why did we fight? Why was her eye fat? Farrell let him know his sister wanted to fight me and that he would have to ask his sister what's up. He let him know he was hot about the situation and his sister had scratched my face badly. It wasn't cool. Farrell said, he wanted me to fight her again in front of the brother so the brother can see for himself who won. That's the thing about Farrell. Most gang members just shoot, but Farrell knew how to fight too. He's the one who taught me.

The whole situation made me feel bad for Farrell. His friends seem like they had started switching up on him, acting funny to him. He's trying to defend me over these girls he either grew up with or had sex with, and they were mad. I didn't care if they didn't like me, but they didn't have to start switching up on him too. I knew it was because I wasn't from that side. Farrell would say, "You are now."

I never tried to get involved in gang business, never asked questions about that stuff. What I didn't know didn't hurt me, although sometimes I still had to deal with it, with dudes pressing Farrell with me around and all.

This wasn't no joke. I would never interfere when someone approached him; I didn't want anyone hurting him.

I guess it came with the territory. There was way more to it than I thought. There was some real undercover snake hating going on. It got to the point that Farrell started saying, screw everybody. He drops those guys and starts hanging out with another one of his homies, whom he called his little protégé.

Farrell took Aaron under his wing, and he favored Farrell a lot. He came along after Farrell's little homies Lempi went away on a ten-year sentence for getting caught up with some stuff.

Farrell took it hard when Lempi went away. He did everything in his power to support him. I remember going to visit him and Farrell said he didn't want us to dress up because he didn't want Lempi thinking he was out here having fun without him. So, we dressed down. Lempi was happy to see us when we got there. Going to see someone in prison is intense, so that was my first and last visit.

Now, I would say Farrell was a bad influence on these young men. He was teaching what he had been taught growing up with the older homies — or shall I say the OGs, being from O'Farrell, Banksters living by the gun. I would hope that if Lempi got anything out of this experience, it would be to get himself together to come home a better person and father.

He went away young. He didn't get to enjoy life. When he was sentenced, his girl Taguhi just had a baby.

It's unfortunate that so many African Americans out here are misled, misguided, mistreated, they grow up in dysfunctional families and don't know anything but the streets, gangs, prostitution and pregnancy. They are young with no support.

We don't get an opportunity to experience what most children of other races have, as far as growing up in a normal environment, living in a nice home with a mom and dad, having some measure of wealth because the adults are working, married, raising their kids and not on drugs. In the homes I saw growing up, if a man does happen to be around, you probably don't know him and he's beating your mom and taking anything, she has, which is nothing.

Most of the time, if you're living in decent conditions in the hood, chances are you're not doing it the right way. You're selling drugs, stealing, committing fraud, or all the above to make a dollar. You're praying you make it home without getting caught, and you've probably already done some type of jail time.

You're a creature of habit and all you know is how to take care of yourself, to just be selfish to survive.

You're not trying to break the cycle. The generational curses keep piling up, and you don't realize that it's affecting your children tremendously.

How does it affect us? We grow up thinking this is normal. We live for material things. We look for love in all the wrong places. Mentally, physically, emotionally, we seek father figures. We're looking to fill that empty void, looking for anyone to fill the spot.

You ain't out there sacrificing and working hard at a job, making decent money, doing what it takes to show your family this is how it's done, and it's not your fault. What is your fault, is not changing yourself for the better?

That explains why most of the time we grow up thinking all this is normal. We know nothing else. We've never seen it. Every dollar we get burns through our pockets. We don't know how to invest. Half of us don't have an education past the sixth-grade level. How are we supposed to help support others and love others when we can't even take care of ourselves?

On those streets in southeast, everybody is in competition. There's no such thing as loyalty. Everybody is for self, and no one wants to see anyone else shine like a star. If it ain't the drugs taking us out, it's the gangs.

We black women can't get along for the life of us. Everyone wants to be better and fake, for whatever reason. We are too busy worrying about all the wrong things. It's crazy and sad how blinded we are by society.

The police take us out enough, but we don't realize that so many of us are taking each other out over all this petty stuff: a color, a neighborhood, a gang sign. We're missing the whole fact that our kids are out here suffering because of our actions.

We go out and try to keep up with the Joneses. We try to make ourselves feel relevant. You need that validation from the streets to keep you going, to make you feel like you are someone.

I can honestly say, everything I went through in my life, I don't regret it today. I can also say, I do wish I had made better choices. The things I decided to do at times I knew wasn't right. I don't know if this makes any sense, but I just didn't listen to my conscience. I didn't care. If there was anything I didn't have that I wanted, I was going to get it by any means necessary. Stealing had gotten old.

I would call myself a professional shoplifter. I would steal right under the sales associate's nose at times. It got to the point that I would fill up a shopping cart with flat screen TVs, microwaves, you name it, and just walk out. I wasn't the type to steal and go sell things for money like most people. I stole all that stuff for me and my sisters.

Mind you, I worked my whole life after I left my job at the theater for stealing. I worked at the San Diego unified school district and I enjoyed it. I always loved kids. When I was growing up, I would say I wanted to be a teacher. I was there for a little over six years until they ran into budget cuts and I got laid off. I started collecting unemployment and got lazy. I didn't start looking for a job right away. I would just go to the mall and steal with all that time I had off. It wasn't a good habit at all.

The turn up is real. Farrell and I eventually got bored with our circle of friends, got bored of doing the same stuff in Tijuana or Rosario. All that got old. We were over it. We had new money and we were looking for a nice time with new people and new things.

Around 2006

We start hanging with my cousin Dada and her boyfriend big Tee and his crew. It was crazy how it all played out. big Tee was an OG from the Lincoln Park Blood Gang.

We had fun partying with them. Anything they did was always big baller status, nothing less. We fit right in. That was the life I cherished back then.

It started to bring a lot of tension Farrell's way. He was hanging with the wrong Blood territory, and his homies were getting jealous because they felt like Farrell wasn't looking out for them anymore, like he'd forgotten about them for these new bloods. We didn't even realize it at the time. We weren't around anymore. If we weren't out partying with the crew, Farrell and I would be doing our own thing in Las Vegas.

We pretty much lived in Vegas. That was our getaway spot. We were always high and wanting to stay high, Vegas was the perfect place for that. It never closed. Plus, Farrell had an older homie who lived in Vegas that he would want to go see named Crazy Blood. He said Crazy Blood was his homie who raised him in the set. Farrell had respect for him.

Me, personally? I never liked him. He seemed like one of those sneaky guys you had to watch all the time. His energy every time I was around was bad. I never got good vibes from him. There was something about his eyes that I saw and I hated.

They looked devilish to me. I told Farrell one day how I felt. He just laughed it off and said that's just how the homie was, Crazy Blood. He continued hanging with him. I did my part by telling him how I felt.

Most of the time, guys don't listen to girls when it comes to their homeboys, which is understandable, I guess. Girls are the same way.

Meanwhile, my mom is trying to get it together. She's still learning. She is grown and pays her own bills, which I guess means you can do what you want to do. My sisters are in high school now, old enough to take care of themselves, too. Conveniently for them, Lincoln High School was walking distance from where my mom was living now. I would always go over and make sure everything was straight.

The thing was, my mom had relapsed, but was hiding it well. She would get high when my sisters were at school and when she knew I wasn't coming over. She did that for a while. Then I started to be able to tell, from her face and how she starts acting. I played the game with her for a while. My sisters knew what was up too.

My dad had start going over there, taking her food and money anytime she needed it. She would watch my brother. It seems like her and my dad had become close. My mom still had my dad wrapped around her finger. You can tell he felt bad for missing out on my life, and she wasn't going to never let him forget. Come to find out, my dad started using too after hooking up with Deana.

I wouldn't have ever thought he was back on drugs. I guess he started hanging out with old friends and family, and temptation got the best of him. It didn't make it any better that he was with Deana. She had her own addiction problem, which probably explains how they hooked up.

It was weird that nobody but me seemed to have a problem with my dad leaving his wife for my uncles' wife. My mom would talk to me about my dad's situation behind his back, but never to him. I would tell her she ought to let him know how she felt.

Uncle Vernus was one of my favorite uncles growing up. He once got shot for robbing a 7-Eleven. This was back when I was younger. The bullet left a hole in his chest and left him paralyzed from the waist down.

I remember getting him gauze to dress the wound on his chest. He was fly for being in a wheelchair. For one, he was handsome from the start. He had long, black, pretty hair, beautiful skin and white teeth. He still had a lot of females even though he was paralyzed. He had a car and everything.

He couldn't operate gas or brake pedals, so he drove with hand controls. I'll never forget it. He would pick me up, take me wherever I wanted to go and buy me whatever I wanted. I would sit right in the middle of him and his girlfriend Deana at the time.

The only thing about Uncle Vernus was, he had the same addiction as his mom and my mom (his sister). He loved pills. And then, the pills started to take him down. He and my mom would do them together. I loved him. I remember helping him a lot growing up, giving him baths, combing his hair, feeding him, whatever he needed.

Out of my mom's brothers, Uncle Vernus and my other uncle Sim were the only ones that didn't have kids. Uncle Sim was kind of weird though. Growing up, I remember him always being in a mental hospital or in jail. I remember when he was around, which wasn't often, he was nice but it always seemed a little strange.

I remember him coming to our house once when we lived in East Diego. My mom had stepped outside for a moment and I was in the bathroom. Then I heard my mom coming in the house saying, "Sim, what the hell are you doing?" I came out the bathroom and he was trying to smell my little sister's you know what. My mom made him leave. I see why he didn't have kids.

My mom had four brothers in all. I love my uncle Bike too. He was a real ladies' man growing up. He was cute, tall, with brown skin and a cool personality. He was fun, always smiling, and had a lot going on for himself. He was good at doing hair. He worked at this shop called Hair Affair in National City, off Plaza.

He would also smoke lots of weed. He had a daughter a few years younger than me, named Sydney, and we were close. I remember him telling me that when he found out his girl was pregnant and having a girl, he said he wanted his daughter to come out looking just like me. That made me happy. And the funny thing is, people thought she really did!

Then there's Uncle Phil. He was the manager of the Jack in the Box on Federal and Euclid, until people he knew robbed him. Then he moved away to Texas with my grandfather and never looked back. This was all when I was still young, but it hurt me to see him go. I loved Uncle Phil.

I was with him so much that his daughter, my older cousin Bree, told me she would hate to see me coming with her dad to her house. She said she would think to herself, "Don't you have a dad. It wasn't my fault. My mom was the only girl among her siblings, and I was the only kid around at my house.

To this day, I don't have close relationships with my blood cousins. My real girl cousins, we barely feel like family to each other. Sometimes I think if maybe our parents had raised us together, we would have been closer.

I know my mom was back using. She has me stressed out. I'm smoking more weed, drinking whatever it takes to numb the pain.

Dad's tripping too. I'm wondering, what's wrong with my parents? It seems like they can't win for losing. Then we find out Deana is pregnant. I'm pissed! I want to tell my dad, you're too old for another kid, and you didn't even raise me.

That's all I remember my grandfather saying when my dad was in prison and he would come bring me money.

I would hate having to call and ask my grandfather (my dad's dad) for money, because I knew his wife hated my dad and everything that came from my grandpa's previous marriage. But my mom would insist. She said he had the money to give. My mom would say my dad's side of the family didn't do anything for me. when I hear the news about Deana and their baby, I'm livid. My dad is still married and he wants me to be happy for him? The audacity. The whole time Deana was pregnant, I make a point of distancing myself from them. I wasn't OK with the situation at all. You can tell my dad was hurt over it. I didn't care.

My mom would always have my little brother. She was his permanent babysitter. Every time she would call my dad for money, which was often, he would ask for her to babysit in return. She had no problem with that. She loved my brother like he was her grandchild. She would watch him even if she were high. It gave her something to do. Her being high stressed me out, but I guess everybody's entitled to live their life the way they want, high or not. I had to remind myself, I have no control over anyone, so let me stop stressing out before I kill myself over these "adults."

Nothing really changes as far as me and Farrell go. We're still partying with the crew, Farrell was selling more weed, he's going to the auction more than usual, buying cars, keeping the ones he likes, fixing them up and selling the ones he didn't. So it goes, back and forth, whatever he wanted to do.

We start going to the mall like crazy. Farrell needs every pair of Jordan sneaker that came out. We would have to be at the mall at 5am so he could be one of the first in line to get the shoes before they sold out. Every store only had a certain number and they went fast. I would hate getting up so early for a pair of shoes. But every time Farrell bought himself a pair, he bought me matching ones, so I couldn't complain. We would look fly, wearing our matching outfits and taking pictures. We were the cutest couple around.

Crazy Blood, the big homie who we would go see in Las Vegas from time to time, had moved back to San Diego and was not doing too good. I guess he gets an earful of what's been going on with Farrell while he was out in Vegas; he thinks Farrell is on and doing it big, got money hanging with these Lincoln dudes.

Whatever the case may be, they're all jealous and hating Farrell in them streets bad. I remember a phone call from Crazy Blood telling Farrell he isn't doing well and he needed Farrell to set him up a lick so he could come up. I tried not to eavesdrop too much, but I would worry about Farrell.

Farrell just continued doing him. I do not think Crazy Blood liked the fact that Farrell was ignoring him, and he was hungry for money. I guess he felt like he had brought Farrell up, that Farrell was his little homie, so when he needed help under any circumstances Farrell is obligated to help. Plus, Farrell hanging with the other side, doing it big, splurging, all that didn't make things look any better. That's how I took it.

Around December 19, 2006

It's my birthday. I remember me and Farrell dressed alike in the same colors, red and green, and dark blue denim. I had a hotel party at the Sheraton in Mission Valley. It was nice. We invited a selected few, smoked weed, chilled, and did whatever else we wanted to do. I remember smoking so much weed that the smoke detector went off.

That night, one of Lamya's homegirls came through to buy some weed from Farrell. I remember thinking it was weird at the time, because I had never seen her buy weed from him before. I tried not to think negative though. I brushed it off, asked him about it, and figured that's all I could do. There was nothing I could blame her for; from what I'd seen she was just buying weed. Besides, she was cool. I really didn't trust females, and that was my own problem.

I did end up hearing something about this girl, who had come to buy weed from Farrell, from my cousin Faas. She said that she had seen her homegirl Melissa at Plaza Bonita mall with Farrell on top of the parking structure looking kind of suspicious.

I was hoping that wasn't true. I knew Melissa well. We had all gone to Lincoln High, and I had even dated her baby daddy before they got together. I thought her friend coming by was quite strange, but I didn't know anything for sure, still not knowing who liked Farrell or not. I still called her homegirl, and her mom and my mom were homegirls growing up, so I would always try and keep the peace with her.

I never said nothing about it. I always laughed with her whenever she was around Lamya. Girls and dudes are scandalous. I knew what Farrell was about; I've been with this man for six years. I knew for sure none of these females would be taking my place, so keep sneaking.

I was truly never worried about anybody taking my place. That was impossible, I thought. I always felt that if Farrell leaves, he never was mine. It was just a trip to me; how other girls were. And when you think about it, when I got with Farrell, lots of girls liked him. I knew what I was signing up for. I wasn't the only one after him; he just happened to fall in love with me.

Anyway, Farrell had a surprise for me after the hotel party. He tells me to pack up, we're going to Vegas. I'm ready. We go to Vegas, have a wonderful time, just me and him. We stay there for a week, celebrating. Even the drive there and back was part of the fun.

We get back, we go out with the crew a few times, and then things are back to usual. Now we are chilling, getting rest and getting ourselves together. We need to detox after partying like fools in Vegas for so many days. During this time, Crazy Blood call about his same situation. He needs money.

Around
January 24, 2007

All I remember was Farrell promised to take me to Red Lobster that day and I really want to go. I don't think it's a good ideal to go meet Crazy Blood, but Farrell decides to go anyways. He's getting dressed, talking, telling me he'll be back by six so we can go eat. I'm not tripping.

I go to Lamya's house to chill in the meantime. We are drinking and smoking, listening to music, joking, doing the norm. I realize it's past 5 o'clock and I haven't heard from Farrell. I call his phone. No answer. I wait a minute, then call again. Same thing. I keep calling back to-back trying to get ahold of him, but still, no answer.

At this point, I don't care if Farrell is with a female, he's going to answer the phone. I'm calling and calling, but nothing. I text him, "Why aren't you answering?" I don't get a response. It's getting later, and I'm getting worried. I call his phone from 5:00pm to 12:00am midnight. At last, someone answers Farrell's phone.

It's Crazy Blood, but I don't know that. All I hear is a man's voice that isn't Farrell. "Hello."

"Hello, who is this and where is Farrell?" I ask, trying to keep the panic out of my voice.

"I don't know. I found this phone on the gas station floor."

"What? On the gas station floor? Where? Can I come get the phone? This is his wife. I need that phone."

"Yeah. I'm a crib from the coast, on 33rd. When you get to the end of the street, call this phone and I'll bring it out."

I thought all this sounded strange because Crips don't talk like that. I have family that's Crips so I know the lingo.

"Okay, I'm on my way." I'm really panicking now. I still don't know what happened to Farrell.

Lamya and I hop in the car and rush down to 33rd. When we get there, I start calling the phone, but now I'm getting no answer again. I call a few more times. The phone's off. I am upset and worried. We drive around for a minute, looking for Farrell or anybody. No sign of Farrell. The streets are super dark and totally deserted.

We go back to Lamya's. I stay there for a while, trying to think of where Farrell could be. I end up going home to see if maybe he made it home but lost his phone or something. Mind you, it's four in the morning now, and still I've had no word or sign from Farrell.

My stomach doesn't feel right. I leave and go to my mom's, tell her what's been going on. Luckily, she wasn't high or had already come down. She tries to convince me that Farrell is okay, that he's probably just out cheating on me.

I had to let her know that's not possible. I don't care if he cheats or not, he's come home to me every night for six years, and that's how I know something's wrong. My mom didn't like Farrell, so I'm not surprised at her being negative.

My sisters are there and Lakeyna tells me, "I seen Farrell yesterday. He was riding past my school and I asked him for a ride, and he told me he would give me a ride but he was on his way to his friend's house."

She said she didn't pay it any mind. She told him it was okay and that she would see him later. She had also seen weed in the center consul, but that was normal so she didn't think anything of it.

I leave my mom's and start driving everywhere I can think of where Farrell might be. There was one house I drove to, on Imperial and 63rd, where I knocked but no one answered the door. I'm backing out, on my way to leave, when I see a girl, I know at the gas station right next to the house I had just left.

Tasha lives in that house with her cousin Davis the same guy that's mad at Farrell over the syrup. I pull up and ask her, "Hey Tasha. Have you seen Farrell?"

Tasha tells me, "No, I haven't seen him," but she says it in a very panicky voice, starting to shed a tear.

"Are you sure? Is everything okay?" I'm out of the car now and give her a hug.

Tasha recovers, "Yeah…I'm okay."

"If you see him, will you let me know please?"

Tasha agrees, and I continue driving around looking for him. I had to call into work to explain that I couldn't find Farrell.

I start driving towards Emerald Hills. Before too long, I spot his homeboy Reed riding by. I manage to flag down Reed and ask him, "Have you seen Farrell?" I let him know something isn't right and I haven't seen him since yesterday.

Reed tells me, "I haven't seen blood yesterday in the set."

I'm super frustrated no one has seen him since, and I'm feeling unsettled by the way Tasha acted. I don't know what's going on. I reach out to Farrell's sister to let her know everything that's going on. She starts helping me look, trying to find him, but she can only help from a distance; she lives in the Bay area at this time.

From there, I call the police. They ask me if it has been 72 hours since he's gone missing yet. It's only been 24 hours at this point, so they told me to call back in 72 hours. From there, his sister puts up a picture on MySpace with a post letting the world know Farrell is missing, along with a description on the car he was in and what he was wearing the last time he was seen.

I'm sick with worry. I can't eat, sleep, smoke weed, drink, none of it is working. Lamya was over my house with me, waiting for Farrell to return.

Seventy-two hours pass, and I call the police to let them know he's still missing. I file a missing person report. Some reporters from a news station show up at my house to interviews me. I'm on the news now. They tell his story, then they posted our pictures. From there, everyone is reaching out, asking what happened, this and that.

Farrell sister is being supportive and staying strong, at the same time she was pregnant. I can't imagine what she was going through.

We leave my house, me, Lamya and Farrell's cousin Sade. We drove to Lamya's house to pick up something, then we drove to Emerald Hills Park to smoke a blunt to try and calm my nerves. It feels like there's nothing we can do.

Shortly after we arrive at the park, Farrell sister calls and tells us someone from MySpace reached out to her and said they had seen the white Dodge Magnum Farrell was in parked on Meadowbrook and Shorewood. That was maybe 10 to15 minutes away, depending on how you drive. It seemed like we got there in five.

I see the car. I hop out as fast as I can. A police officer was arriving to the scene at the same time as us. I run to the car and all I can remember is the two back windows are cracked. I get my hands on the door to try and open it, but the police tell me to step away from the car. I don't want to listen, but I don't want to make things worse either. I think, if only we had arrived one minute sooner. I would have seen Farrell in that car dead. Even know I didn't see him, I felt he was in there.

I lose it from there. I break down completely. It doesn't take long for that whole block to fill up with everybody that knew Farrell. It was crazy. We found Farrell around mid-day and they didn't remove his body until that night. We were there waiting all day.

I saw his body from a distance. I was standing closest to the car.

I was lost for words. My baby is gone. They killed him. Nobody knows anything, and Farrell's in the trunk in a fetal position, stripped down to his boxers and socks, left there for days. It felt like my heart had literally been ripped out.

I didn't know which way to turn. Life with Farrell was all I knew. He had molded me into the woman I was. I needed him. I wasn't ready for it to be over. I couldn't understand what had happened. In the days that followed, I couldn't even eat by myself. I was with Dada and she was bathing me, feeding me, holding me. She was there for me the best way she knew how. I really appreciated that. Without her, I don't know if I would have been able to make it.

Then, it was time to make funeral plans. I would get weak, develop a fever, almost faint and pass out just thinking about it. They would have to do without me sometimes. While going through all that, I also had to prepare to move out of the apartment we shared. Everyone that was around supporting me was helping me organize things to get them in storage.

I was giving Farrell's things away to his close friend and brother who was down from North Carolina. His father had also come in from out of town. He was very rude, nasty and disrespectful. The first thing he did when he walked in the house was go straight to my bedroom, flip over the mattress and said, "Where's the money and guns?"

That shocked the hell out of me. I met his dad one time when we went to visit him out of town for a week and he seemed nice. This guy I met the second time around was someone totally different. I am out of my mind with grief, but how the hell do you come into my house asking where my money is and trying to take things that don't belong to you?

Last I checked, his father put Farrell out of their house, sold it and moved away. The nerve. Come to think of it, his dad didn't even help with the funeral. You would think he would have sympathy regardless of the situation. Sure, he spent his life with me, but that is still your son.

After the funeral, nothing still really felt real. I don't know if it was because I haven't gotten closure or justice hasn't been served or what. I wanted to know who killed Farrell. And who was that who answered his phone? I had end up accessing his voicemail but found nothing connected to his death. All I found was a girl in one message crying her heart out about me, saying all Farrell wants is her money all he loves is me.

I guess she had given him a couple of racks and he had promised her time. They were messing around, this same girl I heard crying was at the club one night. Farrell and I was there separately; I went with my friends and he went with his. I remember her following their crowd. She was a hood rat, so she could have been with the whole set. Farrell liked them hood rats they were easy access.

I was in love with a dead man for about two years. It was so weird. I was still thinking he was going to walk through that door one day. It was a very depressing time. I moved in with my mom and my sisters after that. I felt I really needed to be close to them; I didn't have nobody else.

Then I lived with my cousin Dada for a while. After I left Dada's house, I went to Sade's house with her and her family. Her brother was still down from Iraq for Farrell's funeral. I knew Sade's brother from high school as well. I never knew he liked me, but after Farrell passed, he let me know how he pretty much wants to take care of me for Farrell.

Sade wasn't feeling that at all and it caused tension between us.

I was in a very vulnerable state of mind, so I thought his offer sounded good. I didn't realize I was just going along with the flow. It didn't last long. God worked it out for the better.

After that I would hang back out with my cousin Dada and her husband from time to time. They would try and show me a good time, knowing everything I was going through. I also had my homegirls Aaliyah and Dakila. I would hang out with them from time to time, just to try and take my mind off things. I tried to keep busy.

Shortly after that, I tried returning to work. I knew the money Farrell left behind was going to go fast. It was hard though; I would break down at work sometimes.

I end up going with Dakila and her homegirls to a Superbowl party in these Navy apartments off Home Avenue. That was my first time kicking it with Navy guys. My friend did it all the time. It was something different, and that's why I enjoyed myself. I was tired of being around Skyline. I didn't trust a soul around there anyway. Somebody knew what happened to Farrell, they just weren't saying.

When I was at the Navy party, I end up getting a number from this honey. He was fly and all the girls were on him. I think that's why I got a big kick out of him. I end up leaving that party with him, going to his house to kick it with him and his friends. All his friends called him Rock.

We became cool. We start dating, but I would always still think of Farrell. The only thing that was bad about the situation is when I met this Navy guy, Rock, he lived in Chula Vista, but by the time we start dating, he had moved to the Meadow Brook apartments in Skyline, Farrell's old stomping ground.

I asked him why he was moving over there. I let him know those were the nastiest, most ghetto apartments in Skyline. He wasn't from out here, so he didn't know. I'm thinking in my head, he couldn't come to my house — I was living with my mom in her one-bedroom studio — so we would have to meet up at his. I just had to let him know not to get friendly with the people in his new neighborhood. They can't be trusted, and he wasn't from around there.

One thing about his place was that he made it nice in the inside. He's the first man I ever met who had silk sheets on his bed with candles lit. He was very romantic that way, and he always smelled good and looked good.

Not long after we start dating, I end up getting into a bad car accident with my mom and my youngest sister Trice in the car. Luckily, no one got hurt but me. I broke my nose. I looked like Ricky Racoon for about two months. Rock ends up coming to see me, taking care of me while I was hurt. That really touched my heart that he was there; we hadn't been dating that long. Honestly, I liked him, but I can admit he was a rebound. I was using him to get over Farrell.

I know that wasn't fair to him, so I made sure to keep my distance and not fall in love. Good thing, too, since he had a whole 'another baby somewhere else too. I find this out through a text message in his phone one night when he was drunk asleep. After that, I really start keeping him at arm's reach. I would call and use him when I was drunk.

Unfortunately, those silk sheets, candles and Hennessy got the best of me. Weeks later, I was at my mom's, stressed out, and drunk a whole bottle of wine by myself. My stomach starts to hurt so bad. I run to the bathroom and throw up. My stomach is having, pain like never ever. I tried laying down, thinking it would get better, but it got worse. I told my mom to drive me to Paradise Valley Hospital. I couldn't drive myself.

We get to the hospital, which isn't far from my mom's house, and find out I'm three weeks pregnant. I'm pissed! I made sure that Negro was putting on condoms, but when it comes down to it, I have only myself to blame. There were some nights we were so drunk; I didn't even think to look to see what was going on.

The author (left), her mother (center) and her sisters (back right and center), 2006

Farrell's cemetery 2007

Out on the fire line with some crew members Ashely (left) The author (middle), at Rainbow Camp, 2015.

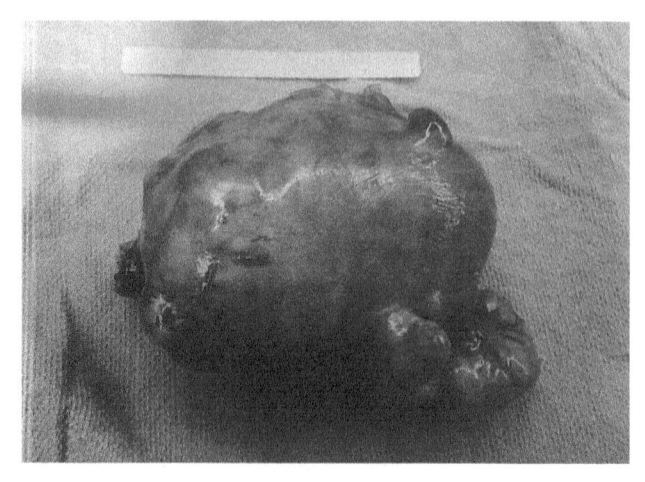

The author's oversized uterus, removed in surgery in 2016.

Obituary and memorial program for the author's father, James Earl, Colbert, 1958-2016

In Loving Memory
Raymond Earnest Robinson

Jun 10, 1957   May 22, 2018

Funeral Service
8 ~ 11:00AM
New Creation Church
?15 Altadena Avenue
San Diego, CA 92105

Memorial for Tooper's father, Raymond Earnest Robinson, 1957-2018. Robinson passed away in hospice while I was changing his diaper.

The author on her wedding day, August 8, 2019.

A proud new driver for UPS, September 2019.

Around 2008

I didn't know what to do. I had never been pregnant by anyone except Farrell. Besides, we had only been dating four months and I just found out he had another baby elsewhere. I'm thinking, this dude got a baby in every state. Navy man. I told Rock what was up. I told him I really didn't want to have the baby and it costed five hundred to get an abortion when it was really forty dollars. He gave me the money and took me to the clinic. He made sure that's what I really wanted to do.

After that, I stopped dating him. I was over it. He wasn't going to have another chance to get me pregnant. I'm out. I felt bad about all these abortions, and I'm still not ready for kids.

After that, I start studying abstinence. I decide that no one is getting any more of this until I'm married and ready for kids. I did that for almost a year.

To occupy my time, I started hanging with my cousin Faas. She would pick me up and get me out the house. We would go to her mom Cookie's house, off Skyline. Cookie was my mom's cousin through marriage. I loved Cookie. Most people who knew her thought she was a mean lady, and she did look a little intimidating, but if you knew her like I did, she was sweet as pie. She always would keep it real. She would always cook great food and feed me when I came around.

I end up moving out of my mom's, into a place with my two home girls

Aaliyah and Rajkumari. Rajkumari was my friend Kay's little sister. We had been close since middle school. We would trade clothes and I would throw mine out my window and over their fence to her.

We move into a three bedroom on Willie James Jones and Imperial Avenue. We had the coolest landlord ever, Mr. Baer. We got into those apartments because Rajumari knew him from living there when she was younger. So, we move in and we all agree that whoever gets the master bedroom must pay more rent since it was bigger and had the bathroom inside. That ends up being me.

My friends were understanding about me needing the space. I already knew what it felt like to have my own place. Me and Farrell had three apartments by then. With, everything cool and everybody got along for the most part. I mean, three women living together, it's never going to be perfect. It helped that we all knew each other prior to moving in.

We decided to have a housewarming party. I don't know what kind of party it was, all I know is that my play brother Mack ended up coming through with one of his homeboys Jacira. My brother was trying to get at Rajumari, and his friend was trying to talk to me. Jacira was very impressive, good looking and fun. I never dated someone who looked like he could be my brother though. I'm light skinned, I tend to like my man dark and chocolate.

That night, I end up going to the store with Jacira. We were just getting to know each other. He had a nice Range Rover and dressed in expensive clothes. His whole look screamed money. Turns out, he knew who I was from Farrell; he had done business with Farrell before. He also knew he was killed. I didn't really want to get involved with that lifestyle again, but I fell right into the trap. Now, Jacira was the one.

I started feeling Jacira fast. This dude would bring me lobster and shrimp for breakfast in bed with champagne. This was on another level. I had never experienced this before, and food is the key to my heart. He was a real woman pleaser.

For not having much family, Jacira was a happy person. He looked at life the best way he could; he never had negative energy. He was a fun person to be around, and he knew how to have real fun. He had multiple nice cars and he would let me drive whichever I wanted. I stayed with good weed to smoke and money in my pockets. Nothing was missing with him. Me and my homegirls would always be partying at his house.

Around 2009

In the process of me dating Jacira, the authorities have a reward out for Farrell's killer. Someone turned him in eight months later. He was out of state with family at the time.

I was happy, thinking things got easier now that the killer was caught. He pleaded not guilty, taking the case to trial. The police end up catching another one of the guys they thought had something to do with it. Someone had overheard people talking the week after Farrell's murder. The last guy they found was Crazy Blood.

He ends up saying he didn't kill Farrell, but he was there. He had just got out from doing 15 years after being involved in a different murder. I let the police know everything I knew about Crazy Blood. I wanted him to go down. He killed the wrong one this time.

I let them know how he was calling Farrell prior to his murder, saying he needed money badly and how he wanted Farrell to set the Mexicans up but Farrell wasn't with it. I told them about how we used to spend time at his house and how Farrell really looked up to him and trusted him.

The trial is starting. I get called up as a witness on the stand. It just got real. You see people coming to court with red stop snitching shirts, ghetto girls with red boots on, representing Skyline and this killer. I'm disgusted.

I must get picked up every morning by the police. I wasn't in protected custody or anything. At first, I told them I didn't fear for my life, that these lame dudes or girls were no threat to me. They had already killed Farrell. What were they going to do, kill me too? I didn't realize how intense it could be, being a witness. That was my first time. I got up on that stand. When it was time to see the body, which they had identified as exhibits A, B, C, and D, and it was Farrell laying there with no clothes on, beat, I couldn't take it. That was my first time seeing him again since he had left the house that day. It felt like it was happening all over again. It was crazy!

Jacira was so supportive and always there for me. I had induced Jacira to my mom. She loved him so much, I thought she wanted to get with him or something. Eventually, I found out he would give her money when I wasn't around, and anybody who gives my mom money is immediately in her good books. He took my sister to Magic Mountain one year for her birthday, bought her whatever she wanted. He was really caring and giving.

When I had a bad week in court, he bought me Keyshia Cole tickets. He knew I loved Keyshia Cole. Rajkumari, Taguhi and I went together and we had a ton of fun. We pulled up in a clean green Navigator truck with our True Religion tailor-made outfits on. You couldn't tell us nothing. And all of it was on Jacira. At the end of the concert, I ran into one of Crazy Blood's girls. She's upset, I guess because the police had a search warrant for her house for bothering and harassing me one day at court with her smart comments. I didn't know the police was going to do all that. All I had seen was one of the officers telling her to shut the fuck up and leave the courtroom.

She ran up, talking at the top of her lungs. It was so embarrassing. I swear, I think Keyshia Cole was watching the drama from the stage. We were right on the side, kind of in front. I scream back, "Shut up! My dude was killed and you trying to fight me. At least you can still see Crazy Blood ugly self!" Like always, I was ready for whatever.

This girl's cousin Shannon was there and she was a friend of mine. The cousin held her back. She's screaming at this point, telling me, "If you gone get off, get off." That's all I'm waiting for. I don't put my hands on no one first; I always let them do their best to me so I can see what there working with and size them up. Nothing happened, thankfully. My homegirl Rajkumari was scared (she's not a fighter), and my cousin Taguhi was nowhere to be found. She was too busy trying to get backstage with Keyshia Cole and Amine, Keyshia Cole's bestie.

The trial goes on for months. There are witnesses that don't want to testify anymore, but still want to be in protected custody. They like the special treatment. Then days, I get fevers and must take breaks. It's so bad I'm throwing up.

Jacira takes me to Los Angeles with him on business. We go to eat and hang out and get away from it all. This was the final day in court when the judge was going to make his decision. Dada went for me. I just couldn't make it myself; it had gotten to be too much. I needed a break.

She calls me with the verdict. A jury convicted Crazy Blood for the second-degree murder of Farrell Walter and found true a criminal street gang allegation. The court sentenced Crazy Blood to an indeterminate term of 15 years to life.

The court's documents tell the full story, and it goes something like this. The following is an adaptation of the court's official record of this case and the appeals cases that followed:

On January 24, 2007, the night Farrell had gone missing, Crazy Blood, Tommie Parker, Carlos Reed, Jamie Davis, and Farrell had gathered with other members and associates of the O'Farrell Park gang in an apartment on 63rd street in San Diego. Among the associates was a man by the name of Smith, who was the first man the police caught and tried and Farrell's murder.

Crazy Blood, called "big homey" by Farrell, was the shot-caller. He had the highest status among members of the O'Farrell Park gang. Smith was also a senior member of the gang. Younger member such as Farrell, Smith and Reed were called the O'Farrell Park Banksters and were lower in the hierarchy. Davis had previously been documented as a member of the Skyline criminal street gang, which was much larger than the O'Farrell Park gang, but he frequented the O'Farrell Park gang territory.

The O'Farrell Park gang was "tight" with Skyline gang; the two gangs "ran together."

Sometime before the killing, Crazy Blood had complained to Smith that he had done favors for Farrell, but Farrell had just looked over him like it was nothing. Farrell drove to the apartment that day in a white Dodge Magnum. The case turns on evidence of what occurred after he arrived, between 1:30 and 2:30 PM on January 24th.

Crazy Blood followed Farrell into the kitchen. As Crazy Blood was getting marijuana from Farrell, Crazy Blood demanded, "Why didn't you answer your phone?"

Smith walked into the kitchen and either he or Crazy Blood asked Farrell, "What are you doing bringing this faggot shit into the neighborhood, fucking with faggots?"

Farrell responded, "That's bullshit. What are you talking about?... You got me fucked up. Fucking with some guys? Are you fucking crazy?"

Crazy Blood and Smith then demanded money from Farrell. Crazy Blood and Farrell began fighting, eventually moving into the living room. At that point, when the fight was one-on-one, Farrell was able to fight back. Smith picked up Farrell's "weed" and money from the floor.

As the fight continued, Crazy Blood and Smith worked together to attack Farrell, telling him not to come back to the neighborhood. When Smith hit Farrell in the face, Farrell fell into the entertainment system, knocking over the television. Farrell called out for Davis to help him.

Davis refused. He joined his girlfriend Richson in their bedroom and one of them turned up the volume of the television. Even over the sound, Richson still heard Farrell screaming and yelling "like a girl."

Carlos Reed entered Davis's bedroom and asked him why he did not intervene to stop his "homies" from tearing up the living room. Davis, who was terribly upset, yelled from the bedroom doorway that everyone had to get out. He did not open the door fully because he didn't want to risk harm to himself or his girlfriend. At one point during the fight, Smith came into Davis bedroom and asked Reed if he had a "whop" meaning a gun; Reed said he did not.

Reed left shortly afterwards and saw that Crazy Blood and Smith had cornered Farrell in the living room. Farrell was alive and fully dressed, Crazy Blood was trying to stop his nose from bleeding, and Reed thought everyone had given up on the fight. He testified that he did not intervene, because "I didn't have no beef with none of these dudes."

When things quieted down, Davis looked out through a crack in the bedroom door. He saw Smith in what he described as an "aggressive stance, like he was thinking, What the hell am I going to do next?" Davis and his girl stayed in the bedroom for what could have been 15 minutes longer before they entered the living room. A lower gang member named Sam was the only person left in the living room.

Later that afternoon, Crazy Blood and Smith returned to the apartment in a white van. Davis refused to let Smith inside. Smith dropped $200 on the ground and said if he had broken something, the money would take care of it.

Farrell sister, Amber, contacted media outlets the next day to report Farrell missing.

She had learned that I, his girlfriend, had not heard from Farrell since the day before. Amber posted her brother's picture and a description of his car on MySpace. com. Colbert had filed a missing person's report with the police. Farrell's body was found in the trunk of the dodge Magnum on January 26, 2007, clothed only in boxer shorts and socks. The medical examiner determined that Farrell died of strangulation.

Investigators collected evidence from the Dodge Magnum, including a bunched-up shirt that appeared to have been used to wipe something down. The shirt had Farrell's blood near the logo and Crazy Blood's DNA on the inside of the collar. A palm print found on the rear bumper belonged to Crazy Blood.

Crazy Blood and Smith were both charged with Farrell's murder, but the court order separate trails with Crazy Blood tried first.

Sam's, Reed, Colbert, Davis and the Richson testified that they and their families had been threatened with retaliation should they appear at the trial. Davis testified that the accusation that Farrell was gay was "obviously bullshit." He had never heard rumors that Farrell was gay. Davis said it seemed like Crazy Blood and Smith were "checking" Farrell. He testified the purpose of checking was "to get somebody's attention...not necessarily to kill them."

Hearing the trial's verdict, I'm so thankful justice has been served. Absolutely no one deserves to be done like that. You must watch who you call friends. The moment someone becomes jealous of you for doing better than them, they want to take it away. Basically, Crazy Blood and Smith took Farrell's life over weed and money. It's not like Farrell was out there like Jay Z; he was just trying to make it the best way he knew how.

Jacira and I are cool. It is going on two years. I'm really feeling him and all the love and support he's been showing has meant everything to me. He's really been there for me. He bought me a white Honda to get around in because I didn't want to drive Farrell's car. Farrell left behind his black Chevy SS and a red Zee, which I sold. I had totaled the PT Cruiser my dad bought me in that car accident with my mom and sister. I would drive Jacira cars but they were all flashy except his one Honda that he would drive around to do his business. I was very thankful he got me that car.

These days, I'm barely at home. I'm always at Jacira's house. I got access to the alarm. I really enjoyed being at his house because he didn't live in the ghetto and his house was nice. Until one night, we go to the grocery store and when we come back and the house is up in flames. The fire department was there and everything. They said he left something near the fireplace and it had caused the fire. Jacira wasn't tripping. He had money and renter's insurance, so it was just on to the next place.

The next place was a house in El Cajon with a pool and a Jacuzzi. I loved that house. Jacira even got me a pit bull. She was super cute. Her coat was a hazel color and her eyes matched. I named her Hazy.

It doesn't take too long for me to find out Jacira ain't all he's cracked up to be. Jacira is a hoe. He's got plenty of women to call. He goes back and forth out of town, from here to there, meeting and greeting.

I go to Los Angeles one weekend to my homegirl Aaliyah's house.

We go to a Lil Wayne and Nicki Minaj concert and I have a blast! It was the best concert I ever been to. Coming home was a whole 'another story.

I come back unexpectedly to find Jacira has a girl and her baby in the house. I went crazy. A hoe turned him on to pimping. He said he knew nothing about it. She told him she wanted to pay him. And that is all she wrote.

It was fun while it lasted. He treated me good, but I should have known it was too good to be true.

After Jacira, I 'm really starting to feel like dating isn't for me right now. It's too much. I haven't even been out of the relationship with Farrell for long, and I could feel it was still too early to really be getting into something else.

I don't even know myself at this point. I feel I was just trying to find love to fill the void that Farrell had left. With that feeling of emptiness inside me, I was so vulnerable. It was easy for me to fall for anybody who came along and did the right thing.

So now I'm living back at the apartment with the girls again and everybody is starting to get on my nerves. Dakila was getting ready to move to her own place, and she didn't stay long. Rajumari and I are starting to argue more than usual. She said I think I ran the house, and this and that. It's not worth my trouble. We can all go our separate ways if we want; this is my first time trying the roommate's thing out anyway.

Things came to a head and Rajumari ends up moving into her own place off Rolando in East Diego. It was a good set-up for her. And we all were still friends, regardless of what went on when we were roommates.

After all the roommates moved out, I'm in the three bedrooms by myself, so I move my mom and my sisters in from there one-bedroom duplex they were in to give them more space and to help my mom out. My sisters were so happy, and their school was right across the street.

Everything was cool until my mom started getting amazingly comfortable and her addiction picked up. She's using extremely heavily and she start stealing from me. I'd find her laid out on the porch, foaming from the mouth. I would have to pick her up, take her to bed and bring her back to life. It was hard, lifting dead weight ain't no joke.

I really couldn't last that long under the weight of my mom's addiction. I was already mentally drained from everything that's been going on in my life. I couldn't handle it. I couldn't let her bring me down so when a one-bedroom came available downstairs that I knew she could afford, I let the owner know she needed somewhere to live. At the same time, I put in my 30-day notice that I would be moving out. He let her move in on December 1, 2009.

I moved to my dad's house in Clairemont, to a condo he was renting from his cousin. My dad is doing good at this point, from what I can see. He's working and just bought a new F150. Everything's good and he's helping me get through. He's cooking for me and we're growing closer.

It hasn't been three weeks since my mom moved into her new place. On December 18, 2009, I get a call. They found my mom dead. I couldn't believe it. I drop the phone. Apparently, my mom had a sugar daddy who also sold her prescription drugs. She was in a hotel room with him and she took too much of the wrong stuff. She didn't wake up.

All I can remember is my mom telling me when she moved in the three-bedroom with me after me and Jacira broke up, she told me, I'm a good strong woman and I deserve a good man, and that someone was going to come along and marry me. I couldn't believe that came out of her mouth. It was the nicest thing she's ever said to me.

I really don't know where to start. My sisters are at school right now. How am I supposed to tell them this? I call my dad hysterical and let him know. He starts crying too. I wait for my dad to get home, then we go to my mom's house and I call a few more people to let them know what happened. They come over to support me.

I go pick up my sisters from Lincoln High School. They can tell somethings wrong because I've been crying. I'll take them back to the house where there are people. I'll let them know things weren't good.

I tell myself I must stay strong for my sisters. I can't cry, and besides, there's too much to do. I must start making funeral arrangements and really woman up to take care of the family. This seems unreal.

I stay at my mom's house with my sisters. The next morning, it is my birthday, December 19.2009 I can't believe it. Mom, not only you passed away, but a day before my birthday.

Not only that, but my sister Keyna is going to graduate this year. She's a senior. This was extremely hard for me. I try to work everything out to where I hope she's happy despite the circumstances.

Around 2010

Shortly after that, we moved out of the one-bedroom into a condominium that came available in Clairemont upstairs from my dad. I was so happy. I loved our new place, and my sisters loved it too. Nice granite counters with the microwave already built-in, stainless-steel refrigerator. We had two bedrooms, two bathrooms, enough space for all of us. We had never lived in anything that nice before — and it wasn't in the ghetto.

On the downside, I did have to drive my sisters to school, which was about 15 minutes away. I had gotten used to waking up on my own time, but it was worth it. I was just trying to make them happy.

I was working for the San Diego School District at this time, but my hours are cut due to budget cuts. I'm collecting unemployment, getting some money for my sisters from the county, but it isn't enough. Trice is a junior and Keyna is a senior. My rent is $1200, plus there are bills to pay.

I'm trying to stay focused at this point and not think about the terrible things I could do to get money. I already had that mindset from stealing at an early age to survive, but I'm trying hard not to go back to my past.

I take a bartending class online, got certified to be a bartender, but I couldn't get a job anywhere because I didn't have any bartending experience. No companies obviously had the time to teach me either.

I'm trying hard to focus on me. I get a membership at 24 Hour Fitness and start job searching. It seems like nobody wants to hire me. To keep my mind occupied, I get on MySpace every now and again.

Through MySpace, one day I reconnect with Tanu. Remember Tanu, the guy who was in love with me in high school? Well after high school, he ended up going away to play college football.

We reconnect on MySpace after all these years. I couldn't believe he started talking to me again. He started to hate my guts during our senior year because of Farrell. He invites me to Vegas for his birthday in February.

I go with a couple other friends from high school to celebrate with him. I don't know what his intentions were, but I knew he was getting out of a long-term relationship. Whatever it was, he ends up asking me to marry him while we were there! All I could think of were my mom's last words, telling me how I was a good woman.

I was very vulnerable, overwhelmed and grieving at this point. My mom had just died in December. Since then, I had been constantly working, from making funeral arrangements and moving to taking care of my sisters and trying to find a job, all while keeping myself together somehow.

I said yes. It felt like a dream come true, like a fairy tale. It was weird because we knew each other but we didn't ever date. We had just start talking on MySpace after seeing each other in high school. That was literally about seven years ago.

Once I said yes, he wants to get married the next day. This was Vegas, after all. I don't know what was going through my head. I was just going with the flow. We get married. We end up having sex for the first time on our honeymoon.

I called my dad and let them know I'm married. He didn't believe me. He didn't know Tanu. I had never introduced him, so the only time he had seen Tanu was when I sent him that picture of me and Tanu at a dance. My mom had liked the picture, but my dad didn't like the fact Tanu had his hand on my butt.

Come to find out, my dad and his mom were good friends. They had done drugs together in the past. And his mom knew my mama from dating the same guy once upon a time, the guy who would help my mom out but whose brother tried to pay me for sex growing up. Small world.

When we get back to San Diego, Tanu moves out of the place he had been sharing with a roommate in Spring Valley and moved in with me and my sisters in Clairemont. Everybody just can't believe it was so sudden. Honestly, I couldn't quite believe it either.

Looking back, I can honestly say I didn't even love this man or really know him. Our relationship turned out to be a disaster. It got to the point that he bought a refrigerator to put it in my room because he didn't want my sisters eating the food he would buy. He didn't like my dad, and my dad didn't like him either. My dad used to joke around and say, he was going to come home one day and my house was going to be yellow taped off. You know what that means. My little brother would ask Tanu to play his games; Tanu would tell him no.

One thing I learned is to never marry a man who disrespects his mother, and Tanu was so mean and disrespectful to his mom. He held a lot of resentment toward her. Growing up, most of our parents was crackheads, but he couldn't let it go. I tried to tell him, just be happy she's alive today trying to have a relationship with you.

I had just lost my mom to drugs; I can't take that he was very insensitive to that situation. I remember my first Mother's Day without my mom. I was at work stressing out. I can't remember who called whom first, but Tanu and I ended up on the phone and I was crying, and he just went off on me for whatever reason, saying things like, how was he supposed to know I'm down and out about my mom? He basically told me, she's been dead already, so why am I still bothered?

He played a lot of mind games. He had a degree in psychology. We stay married almost one year, but it got bad. I knew he was going to start getting abusive after he poured beer on my head that first time trying to address a serious situation about a child, I heard he had. He was buff, too. I couldn't risk getting beat by him. I start sleeping on the couch and doing my own thing. He wanted to start going to counseling and trying to work things out, but I didn't think it was worth it. I didn't love him. I wasn't in love it's time for me to move on.

He was giving me a tough time with the divorce —technically, it was an annulment, because we weren't married long. I wanted to get it done by any means necessary, and he hates me for that. But I'm fed up and determined. He must go. He says he wants to work on our marriage, but I see no change in him and I wasn't trying to change a grown man. I needed him to be ready already, or I knew he would never be for me.

Once that was done, I didn't want to date any more dudes around my age. In my eyes, they were all just dumb, immature, want to be controlling and not ready for a meaningful relationship.

Around 2011

I got bored, distracted, and I need money. Tanu and I were going half on all the bills, but now it's just me again. In the mist of that, I'm on MySpace again and I reach out to this guy I knew through my cousin Faas. He was a truck driver and word on the street is, he liked younger girls and didn't mind paying for them.

I know my cousin and a couple of her friends had him. I'm cute so I think, let me see what I got. He ends up giving me more money than I expected just for an Internet chat. I'm thinking, I like you! You put your money where your mouth is. Actions speak louder than words, and I like what you've got to say.

We became cool. Thanks to my relationship with him, I had a Mustang, a Camry, a Navigator, a Challenger — whatever I needed, he was there. And the best part is, I never really saw him since he was always on the road.

It was the best arrangement ever.

My sisters were learning how to drive, so they would drive the Camry to school sometimes. Until Lakeyna was being sneaky and got in a car accident and didn't tell me

I don't understand why I start getting so money hungry and materialistic. I mean, I've always had pleasant things once I was able to get them for myself. But lately, it had gotten bad. I was at the mall buying

Louis Vuitton purses, and I was in the hair salon every Friday. I stayed in name brand clothes and shoes.

I don't know what possessed me to start thinking about robbery. I literally started thinking about how to case out a bank. "Set It Off" was always one of my favorite movies. I knew I didn't have any friends to help me pull off something like that, so it was going to have to be by myself. If that were the case, my thoughts would stay a daydream.

Unfortunately, the thought escaped my mind because I ended up meeting Fly. This was a guy I met through my cousin Dada at his birthday party in Mission Valley at Mr. O's, which is now a Broken Yolk.

Fly was a married man, and I wasn't going to break up an untroubled home. I was younger than everybody at the party. His homeboy was trying to get with me, and I think Fly saw that, so he let my cousin know he wanted me. He felt comfortable telling Dada because they grew up together and they called each other brother and sister. Obviously, my cousin knew he cheats on his wife.

She tells me that he's feeling me. I ask her, "Ain't that his wife over there, sitting at the table staring over here? He's drunk, cousin. I'm a new cute face around. He'll get over me when the alcohol wears off." Apparently not.

Somehow, someway, my cousin convinces me to go out on a date with him. I'm stupid. He wasn't even cute to me when I had seen him, and he was little. He had swag though. We go on our first date in La Mesa. We go for lunch at a Mexican restaurant right off the Grossmont freeway exit.

I remember what I was wearing and everything. I remember how he looked too. I wasn't convinced the first date, but he was cool, I guess.

One date led to four years. Do not ask me how in the hell my stupid self-fell in love with a married man. It went on so long that eventually his wife found out. I'm going to leave it at that.

I still have money from the truck driver friend on the side. I'm still buying Yorkie Terriers, including one we named Cash, because that's what he cost! Me and my sister's treated that dog like he was a human. He got groomed every two weeks and got his teeth brushed; he stayed fitted, had his cologne, and we took him around in a stroller. He was lazy. I don't look at this trucker like my boyfriend or anything; we were just cool friends.

One morning, Keyna, Trice and I go to Mamie's Cafe in Mission Valley for breakfast. It was raining hard on our way back home. We were on Interstate 805, going north in the fast lane. I was driving a black Mustang. A big rig drove by and splashed a ton of water into my lane, and we hydroplaned all the way across traffic into the slow lane. Trice was in the back seat. The window shattered in her face. Keyna had passed out. I didn't know what to do. When we came to a stop, I dragged Trice out of the back seat. I see so much blood. She was still conscious, but I knew she was hurt and bleeding bad.

God sends a registered nurse to the scene to help me. She already called the police. She tells me to go help Keyna, and that's what I did while she took care of Trice. It was a traumatic experience. I was so blessed the paramedics arrived quickly, and we were right by Children's Hospital.

Latrice had a contusion over her right eye. They stitched her up and said she would be all right. Thank God. If the glass had hit any closer to her eye, it would have been far worse. I felt so bad. I am blessed God was on my side.

In my last few years in the relationship with Fly, I stop really paying the truck driver any attention, so the money wasn't as good. Plus, my job laid me off completely. I felt like I needed four incomes at this point.

My first robbery, I got away with the diamonds. I got what I needed plus some and got out of there unharmed. The only thing I felt bad about was having my sister Keyna be my getaway driver. If we had gotten caught, of course, I would have taken the blame. But if things hadn't gone as planned and something had gone wrong, I would not have been able to live with myself.

When I went home after the robbery and told my dad what I did, he said he had just seen me on the news and that he couldn't believe that was me. With a smirk on his face, he said, "You're just like your daddy, girl."

That didn't stop me. I pulled off another one a few months later. This time, I went alone. I wasn't making the mistake taking my sister again; if I had to, I would go down alone.

That one was so easy, easier than I expected. I was thankful for that. I got what I needed and got out of there. That one didn't make the news, and I didn't have to do what I did at the first robbery. In fact, it was so simple that I wanted to do another one right after that because I didn't have to show a weapon this time.

Nobody knew what I was doing except my sisters and my dad. My dad would give me pointers on what to do better.

I started to get extremely comfortable with robbing at this point. I was thinking, I'm ready to take a bank. But I wanted to do one more thing before going after a bank, just to prepare myself and make sure I'm ready.

Maeva worked at a bank at this time. I started asking her questions about her job, really trying to figure out the inner workings of the place.

I'm partying, going out with my auntie Janan, living it up. She knows where to party. I'm doing all this trying to shake the feeling that Fly's wife found out about us. I'm really putting myself in her shoes and feeling like trash. I'm torn in between the two; I'm not trying to throw him under the bus, but this is spouses we're talking about. I want out. I'm hurting myself and I don't like that I'm hurting her.

One evening, Auntie Janan and I were at a cool bar on Euclid called Tina's that mostly catered to the older crowd. As I'm on my way to the bathroom, this fine older man ends up attracting my attention. I made sure he noticed me. It worked. As soon as he sees me, he said, "excuse me" and grabbed my arm. I smiled. He asks me what I'm drinking. I told him Hennessy he said that's "my kind of girl." That's what he drinks. I'm thinking to myself, okay, old daddy. His name was Mel.

We went back to where my auntie Janan was sitting. She knows this man; he was married to her friend in the past. Damn, everybody knows everybody in southeast, I'm thinking to myself, but if this man ain't still married, he might have action. I ain't going through that again. There are too many men out here for that.

Auntie Janan didn't get in my way. She even filled me in on him. It's whatever at this point, I'll see what I can see.

After he found out my age and that I didn't have kids, that I was an alcoholic like him and that I could cook, he was mine. He once told me, a key to a man's heart is through his stomach. He loved my fried chicken and coming over to my house to a fully stocked liquor cabinet. I kept it filled with the best.

He was cool, for what it was worth, showing me different things, helping me forget about Fly. The only thing was, I was never a fan of being on the back of motorcycles, and motorcycles were his passion. I was the type that like to stay cute and roll a nice car. I didn't want to wear a helmet on my head all the time. My hair is always done. I got tired of it being messed up, after paying all that money getting it done wearing boots and jackets. Don't get me wrong, Harley girl clothing is cute sometimes, but it wasn't the look for me all the time.

Plus, half of the time we were riding we were under the influence. How safe is that? I refuse to be a crash dummy. I remember, one day, I fell asleep on the freeway coming back from a bar and he didn't even realize I was asleep until we stop at a light and my body flew forward.

I would have to see Fly sometimes. Him and Mel were both in the motorcycle scene, but from different clubs. When I asked Mel if he knew Fly, he would act like he started the motorcycle scene. Mel was originally from Los Angeles and didn't know any of them new dudes in San Diego. He said he would see them in passing, but that was it. He stayed with his main riders, and everyone else rode with theirs. I was cool with that.

I let Mel know about Fly, so there wouldn't ever be any surprises. I let him know he was a mistake and I told him about the whole situation that took place. Mel wasn't feeling what I had told him. I asked him, does that make him look at me any different? He said it was all good. He was still feeling me. Then he asked, "Are we done with this?" I said, "Thanks to you, baby, you are making it easy for me."

Fly would say slick things to me, like I'm with an old man. I replied,

"All you old men are all the same, you try and act young to get younger girls. So shut up, Fly, and stop hating on me and my new boo thang."

Man, or no man, I still need real money. I've still got the truck driver friend every now and again, but it's just a bit on the side. Mel had found out about Pay and things got ugly. I need a break from all these dudes. I need to focus on my robbery. Everyone wants my time, but I don't have it to give unless we're talking big.

Latrice is graduating soon. I must get her ready for prom and all the senior festivities that are coming up. I stole her dress from this dress store in Grossmont. The dress was too big, so I had to take it to get it resized. I end up taking it to this Hispanic lady name Rosie, who I met through Taguhi a few years ago. She was a genuinely nice lady. She lived off Federal but ends up getting evicted during the time she's working on the dress.

Dada and I go to her house and see the padlock on the door. We looked through the window and see the dress on the sewing table. I bust the window open and get the dress, praying it was finished. God is good; the dress is done. Even better, it all worked out that I didn't end up paying to get tailored. I'm broke with no help.

I start distancing myself from Mel. He started to become a stalker, following me, putting his direct hand on me. It got out of hand. I remember, one night, he didn't want me to leave. We were arguing and I was over it. I had a home to go to, so I get up to leave. He chased after me all the way to my car with nothing on but boxers. I'm so glad I got away that night.

He's yelling after me, calling me a liar and all kinds of bitches

I tell him, Your way too old for this. Who cares if I'm lying? You knew that from the start. I told you I didn't want to be in a relationship when I met you. I just wanted to have fun and kick it, no strings attached. I was all confused at this point. I need to get myself together. You start putting claims on me without my permission. That's your fault. You knew what you signed up for; I'm 23 years younger than you. Those are the consequences you pay for messing with someone that much younger than you.

He didn't get it. I was young and tender, vulnerable. He said I was the youngest he had ever had. Mel was a character.

Keyshia Cole was coming back in town. She was going to be at Humphrey's by the Bay. Mel bought me tickets. He said I wasn't acting right, and he took them back. I had someone else buy the tickets then and went with my auntie Janan. We're about to sit down and my aunt notices Mel with a girl going to sit in the third row. He took someone else with the tickets he bought for me. I walked over there to make sure he sees me and introduced myself to the lady as Lacole. Mel corrects me and says, "my woman." I walk away and tell them both to enjoy themselves. Mel follows me to my seat and ask my aunt to trade seats with him. She says no. You can tell his date wasn't feeling him after that. Shortly after he arrives back to his seat, they leave. Aunt Janan and I stayed and enjoyed the concert.

Mel was the first man to ever put a gun to my head. I'm thinking older man were cool, but they're crazy too. I can't get a good man for the life of me. I should have recognized from the start when he started trying to control who I spent time with.

My dad hated the fact that I dated him. He was one year older or younger than my dad, but they were the same age. He would say about Mel, "How would he feel if I dated his daughter?" I never told my dad that Mel had put his hands on me before.

I functioned as if I didn't have feelings for Mel, but deep down inside, I did. He ended up getting into a bad motorcycle accident coming back from out of town once. He broke ribs and everything. I remember getting the call from the hospital in El Paso, Texas, letting me know how severe it was. I was on the next flight out. I made sure he got home safely and brought him back to life. His recovery took some time because he was old, but he was active so that helped.

Latrice decided to join the army after graduation. At first, she was indecisive, not knowing what she wanted to do. I knew she was a lost young girl. She had lost her mother incredibly young and had no father figure in her life, just me trying to raise her as best as I could. I explained to her she could get a job like everyone else at the mall, or whatever you do when you graduate if you don't go to college, but this was an opportunity for her to get out of the hood and see something different, to travel the world if nothing else. I didn't have that choice. I told her, even if you don't feel it's for you, at least you tried it to know, and all you must do then is not reenlist. Years go by fast.

I moved off Balboa to Clairemont an exit over, into a studio in a complex called Mesa Villas. I had to kick Keyna out; she was being way too defiant and disrespectful, doing too much. I told her, "You are acting grown, go be grown on your own."

Around October 3, 2012

I go inside a payday advance across the street from my apartments.

I go in there disguised as a professional woman, dressed nice and demanding money. I told the woman working behind the counter there was someone waiting for her if she does anything wrong. I know that this money isn't worth her life. "Give me everything you have, then go sit on the floor and wait until I'm out. Wait for three minutes before you get up."

She did just that. After I get the money, I go out the front door, go to the right through the back door of a laundromat. I remove the professional clothes I had on and put them in my purse. I had on different clothes underneath. I walk home. Another one down, another one to go.

I hurry up to go in the house, take my wig and makeup off. I change my clothes, then I count the money. It's only $950. I was sick to my stomach. I usually got way more than that. I'm used to getting thousands.

I didn't do my homework on how much money they carry. This wasn't my ideal robbery. I had taken advantage of the situation for the simple fact that I was in that strip mall earlier that morning, washing clothes at the laundromat.

I see the same girl clerk pull up whom I normally do business with when I get my money orders or Western Union wire transfers. An older man is normally inside with her.

But this morning, the girl goes to open the payday advance with a new boy who looks as young as her. I was keeping an eye out on it during the day. I had an interview at the nursing home at 2:00pm right across the street from the strip mall, so I knew everything had to be timed right if I was going to do it.

I end up leaving. I was done washing the clothes and I had to get ready for my interview. After the interview, I was sure they weren't gone hire me for some reason. I didn't think I had enough experience to work there, and they wouldn't want to teach me.

As I leave the nursing home, I go back to the strip mall and notice the boy who had come in with the girl this morning is leaving. That was my perfect time to do it. So, I do — all for less than a grand. That's what I get. She played me or just did a drop. This couldn't be real. I had more money than that in my purse.

I leave the house mad to get my car. I hadn't intended on leaving my car there, but I ended up driving when I should have walked to the scene. That was the original plan.

When I was leaving out the door after the robbery, I had a feeling that I shouldn't walked to my car, so I didn't.

I get back to my car and get in to leave. As I'm leaving, I see the police entering the parking lot. I'm not thinking anything of it. I go on my way like nothing happened, driving out of the parking lot.

Leaving the parking lot, the police pull out behind me. He lets me drive about a half a mile before he turns his sirens on. I pull over at the Argo gas station right off the 805 on Clairemont.

He asked me if I knew anything about a robbery at the payday advance in the strip mall I had just left. It's the description of my car, but I don't fit the description.

I said, "No officer, there are a lot of silver Challengers in Clairemont with rims. In fact, there's one that lives down the street from me that looks exactly like this one."

I don't know if he's buying it or not. He's there with me for a while alone, then another officer arrives. From there, they explain the situation and tell me they're going to bring the girl from the payday advance to identify if it was me or not. I was a little nervous, but I am trying not to show it.

The girl pulls up in another police car. She said it's not me. I asked the officer if I can go now. He was about to let me go, until a sergeant arrived at the scene. I guess the SDG&E (San Diego Gas & Electric) man who was working on the pole next to the mall told the sergeant the same girl who got out the Challenger was the same girl he saw go into the payday advance. They want to take me down for questioning.

My dad later told me, where I messed up at, I was doing too much talking. They booked me for second-degree robbery and use of a firearm.

I bailed out and plead not guilty, fighting my case from the outs for about nine months. They found me guilty and gave me five years with 85% — two years for the robbery, three years for the firearm, with a 10-year enhancement.

I asked the judge for a 90-day extension. She wasn't having it; she gave me three weeks.

Luckily, I had put in my 30-day notice prior to my court date. I had moved out of Clairemont to El Cajon city after the robbery, it was a lot cheaper, and I needed the space. I was letting Keyna come back home.

She didn't get any better. She was still a hot mess, if not worse, doing the same thing that had gotten me in trouble. One of her boyfriends at this time helped me move into my apartment in El Cajon and robbed the neighbors in the process. I couldn't believe it. All I remember is helicopters flying over the building, police circling in the parking lot, and me not knowing what's going on.

I'm livid! He didn't know I was out on bail for robbery. I'm already hot as a tamale and now you're bringing this smoke to my new house. Oh, hell no! You've got to go, and don't ever come back. I don't need attention like that around me, or thieves. There's only room for one of us.

I'm stressed out. I'm not eating, not sleeping. I know I'm going to do five years in prison.

I'm worried about my sister, how she was going to be living. There's just a lot on my mind. In the process of all this, I let Fly slip back into my life. He didn't know what was going on. I would just kick it with him to try and keep my mind occupied when I wanted to do something else besides Mel.

I get everything pretty arranged for me to turn myself in. I go to the swap meet and sell lots of my things. I put everything else in storage for my sister; she said she's going to get a place. I get my housing deposit back so when I'm gone, it will deposit in my account for Keyna. She has all my information to do what she needs to do.

I had also gotten my second DUI on July 4, 2013, taking Mel home from the beach after watching fireworks. That I had to take care of, since I was bailed out.

Around August 23, 2013

My sister drives me down to the San Diego courthouse. My time to be there is 1:30 PM. I got there about 1:45 PM. I didn't want my sister seeing me like that, so we said our goodbyes in the car. We already couldn't stop crying. Then, I had to go. I was ready to get this over with.

My attorney is there waiting for me. When I arrive, he sits me down and tells me he sees it in my eyes there's someone in heaven watching over me. He can tell I'm a good person who just made a wrong decision, and I was going to be okay. Do my time, get out, and don't look back. That brought tears to my eyes.

I'm sitting there alone waiting to be called when someone walks behind me and rubs my back. I turn and look. It's Mel. I had confessed everything to him before I turned myself in. He asked me if I feel better for telling him the truth. He says he knew it already.

I let him know I was relieved, and that I didn't expect him to stay. Honestly, I didn't really want him to. I wanted to go to prison and not have to think about whether someone was cheating on me or not.

He told me that he respects me for telling him the truth and he loves me enough to wait for me. He hugged me and kissed me.

They call my name. I give him one last hug. The judge reads me my rights and gives me my sentence. The ride to Las Colinas Detention Facility seemed like the longest ride ever. I was in a state of shock. I didn't stay in the county facility for long. I was there in B housing, which is maximum-security housing, for about two weeks.

Being there this time was a quite dissimilar experience from being in there from my DUIs and the very first time I went with Taguhi when we got caught stealing. I had these two cool roommates, so that made it all right. Only one Samoan girl was trying to eat this vagina; she was cute too, but my mind wasn't on that.

Mel would see me while I was in Las Colinas. When he comes to see me, all he talks about is the past and what I did. I'm thinking to myself, I thought you forgave me. I didn't really believe his heart was in it anymore. I was going away, and we had been through a lot in the two years we've known each other. He felt bad leaving right at that moment after telling me he was there for me.

Colbert, roll up! My two roommates both were sad. Cali Koo and Sarah. They start crying, hugging me, singing "The End of the Road" by Boyz II Men. One of my roommates thought I was the nicest person. She said I wasn't made for prison. She said she has never been to prison, and she's always in trouble but they only give her county time.

It's time for me to go to Chowchilla and start my prison sentence. The ride there was even longer than the first, and this time I'm shackled. All I can remember is it being super cold. The air-condition was turned on high on the bus, and we were in very thin Mumu dresses and prison sandals. And just pray you don't have to go to the restroom. We left at around 1:00 AM and the ride was about eight hours north. It really sucked!

We finally pull up to the prison and all of us are ordered off the bus. We all look busted after that ride, and things were about to get worse. You can't have braids in your hair or anything here. Our first stop was Receiving. It's super dirty, the whole place stinks, it's cold, and we're sitting on metal benches, hungry, and we still must wait hours before we get housed. It's a prolonged process, and it's just the start.

I finally get housed. I go in and I can't believe what I'm seeing It's worse than the movies. Then I hear someone shout out, "Coley!" I'm looking all over the place because the place is two-tiered, top, and bottom, and you don't know where the noise is coming from. I finally see who's calling me and it's Lina, Keyna's best friend. I was happy to see her, but not under those circumstances.

This place was all bad. You couldn't use the phone, they barely let you shower or even come out of your cell.

Luckily, I had the luxury to be a porter which was cool because it was only three women out of two hundred women that got this position and this position allowed you to shower when you want and use the phone. I was blessed!

It took you a month to get to shop at the canteen. The canteen had everything good that you can think of, and I love sweets. it was great, except for the fact that you couldn't go to the store to pick or get anything for yourself. I was very thankful for everyone that supported me while I was in prison. It was a blessing; without money on your books, it's hard in there.

I'm put on C yard. They say C yard was the best yard for that prison. That was the highest-level woman's prison they had. I happened to get the ghettoes drug room in the building. That sounds about right.

As I'm walking in the room, the other women are telling me I can't be there. The bed I'd been assigned was taken by someone who was "in sea over sea." What that means is, when an inmate continues to act up, they take everything away and place her in another cell, with inmates that are either sprung out on drugs or bad, so basically, it's jail inside of jail.

I tell these other women, "For real? Y'all got to work that out with the police. This is where they said I'm housed." One of the girls tells me I can stay until they find me somewhere else to go. I said that's fine if you find me somewhere to go. Rumor was when you got over the wall, they will try and punk you and make you even sleep in the hallway. That wasn't going to be me, I'm sorry.

The room was turned all the way up when I entered. There was music bumping loud, cooking, the girls had on make up even better than girls on the street.

It was an eight-woman cell with four sets of bunk beds, four lockers and if you didn't get a locker, you had a small drawer underneath your bunk. The bathroom and shower were together and wide open, where others can see you. It was horrible and crowded but I knew this was something I will have to get familiar with.

I was in the room with all Latinas except two other black girls. By a crazy stroke of happenstance, one of the black girls Ciara was the baby momma of one of the guys who had been in the house when Farrell was killed. What was the odds of that?

Everyone in the room is supposed to have cleaning duty one day a week. Unfortunately, people were getting punk, so you might get more then one day to clean. And by cleaning, I mean you're scrubbing bricks. That wasn't going to be me either.

Me and Ciara became cool. She knew what they did to Farrell was wrong. I couldn't be mad at her anyway; her baby daddy was one of the ones who cooperated with the police.

The other black lady Michelle shared the bunk with me. She was an older lady from Los Angeles and seemed a little off. That wasn't her first term in prison. Anyway, one day, she came in upset, taking it out on me out of everybody. She's talking crap!

She was frustrated that all the roommates were trying to get her out the cell prior to me moving in. They were calling her a snitch. I didn't know the story. Michelle and I had been alright up to this point. I had even shared with her things about my past and my mom passing away. I was new and that made me mutual with everybody. All I would do is read my Bible, eat my snacks, and mind my own business. There was a lot going on in that room. I saw everything from a troubled relationship, people up all night doing drugs, even someone getting jumped on badly. I see why my old roommates didn't think I was ready for this.

But today, Michelle looks at me and says, "Fuck you, bitch. You and your mom are a hoe."

I said, "What did you say?"

I get off my bunk we are in each other faces. I spit in her face. We start fighting. She was huge, about two of me, but I didn't do bad. I held my own. Afterward, my lip was bleeding, but that's about it.

Everybody in the room respected me after that and had my back. They didn't want me moving out of the room suddenly.

Luckily, I didn't get in trouble for that fight or spitting in her face. That's a whole 'another charge. If I had, that could have added more time to my sentence. Michelle admitted to the police that she had been picking on me and wasn't having a good day. She shared that she had tried reaching out to her family through this program called Friends Outside with her counselor, and they didn't want anything to do with her. They rejected her, and the hurt made her angry.

She said I was the nicest girl in the room. I braid her hair and give her food. I stay to myself. She doesn't know what came over her, and she didn't know I was going to snap back. She apologized. Everybody was happy they moved her out the room after the fight.

While all this was happening, they came to bring me a deceit. A deceit was your pass out. It said I was transferring to another prison, the California Institution for Women (CIW) in Corona. CIW is a lower-level prison; they had lowered my custody level. God is good. They say the wait to get in CIW was typically four to six months. I was at Chowchilla for about three to four weeks. It was my time to move on.

I was happy that CIW was closer to home for me. I felt homesick all the way up here in the north. I knew I would never get visitors here. The only thing I was dreading was the long ride back. I didn't feel like being shackled and cold all over again.

The California Institution for Women was the best prison to be at if you're doing time. The visits there was cool. Mel would come every other weekend in the beginning if he could make it. I remember my first unexpected visitor was my "twin" Bree. We call each other twins because we have the same birthday.

She lived close to CIW, so she thought to reach out.

I remember they got Common to come out to do a concert for us. It was so amazing. I will always love and respect him for coming into that prison, making us women feel special in a time like that.

I got to live in the honor dorm, which put me with all the lifers and long-termers. I had the best roommate ever, Ms. Gee. She was an older beautiful white lady who was serving a life sentence. She had already been in for 28 years for something with the cartel.

She had a son my age, and she would treat me like a daughter. She would cook for me. I wasn't good at making prison food. There were times I would eat zoom-zooms and wham-whams, meaning junk food; my sister Trice and my dad made sure I didn't go without.

CIW was different from Chowchilla. It was smaller and set up like a college campus. It was a lot cleaner and divided into two-man cells. I loved living with one roommate as opposed to eight, especially since you went in not knowing these people. It was much easier to get used to. The church there was amazing.

Unfortunately, Mel was there for me for about a year while I was away. I called one night and he was expecting company. He couldn't really talk once they arrived. He said it was his homeboy, there to talk about his wedding. I get it... It is 9:30 pm. I'm calling collect. You don't have fifteen minutes. Your homeboy can't wait. Obviously not.

I start accusing him of tossing me aside. He didn't like it. He said he felt he had to move on, which was simply fine to me. A woman's intuition is never wrong. I really wasn't expecting him to wait anyway. He was already old, and honestly, I didn't know if the woman I was becoming would still be feeling him five years later.

I'm not going to lie, the feeling of someone leaving you when you're in a place like that isn't a good feeling. All I can think is, this must be karma; I had done a lot of serious stuff.

That gave me a reason to get closer to God. I didn't have any more distractions. I end up getting baptized. I joined the choir, dance praised, and only surrounded myself with people that were in fellowship and worshipped in church with positive energy.

Not too long after, Lamya decides to reach out. Prior to me going to jail, we weren't talking, due to drama. I was surprised and happy at the same time to hear from her. We caught up and began repairing our ties.

Around August 20, 2015

I spent about two years at CIW. I was good during that time, so they drop my custody level again, and now I could go to Fire Camp. Fire Camp is a program run by the California Department of Forestry and Fire Protection that brings non-violent, minimal custody inmates to training camps to train as firefighters, and I heard it was the place to be. There was better food and living conditions. It's not a bad place to do your time, but Fire Camp wasn't offered to violent offenders, so not everyone could transfer there.

I was ready to go. The only thing was the physical fitness training (PFT) training was so hard.

I was bleeding nonstop when I got to prison. It was like my period never stopped. I was on iron pills, anemic, and in excruciating pain. I had multiple fibroids in my uterus, and they were trying to Band-Aid it up with birth control pills and shots, but that only made it worse. One day they gave me a shot.

I was raining blood; I would fill up a pad in ten minutes. It was to the point I was in so much pain I couldn't even make it to the toilet. My roommate had gotten scared and called 222, the emergency code in prison. She said it wasn't like me to leave any blood behind. I couldn't help it; my uterus was on fire. I couldn't even stand.

My condition had deteriorated to the point that they had to send me to the real hospital outside of prison. But God got me through. I passed PFT, graduated, and went to camp. I went to Rainbow Camp in Fallbrook Fire Camp is an experience I will never forget. The best parts about it were saving lives, and the meals. We would go to In-N-Out and Denny's when we were traveling on the road, are camp site food was great. At Fire Camp, your family could bring you food from home too.

Auntie Kamal would visit me all the time. She was cool, hooking me up with good meals and desserts.

If it weren't for the food and the chance to do meaningful work, I could've stayed at CIW. Fire Camp was the hardest work of my life. You're out there on the fire lines for 24 hours, hiking, digging trenches, sleeping, shitting, changing pads, whatever there is to do. You're in the mountains, and the fires are your life, and you're doing it whether you like it or not. You are a number and the state owns you, so you're doing just what they say and how they say it, period.

Sometimes I would cry *and* they would threaten to send me back to prison. *By that point,* I didn't care! Luckily, I had this one cute, tall, corn-fed white girl name Ashely *with me*. She was from San Diego; her kids were mixed. It wasn't her first *rodeo.* She knew the *ins* and outs, and she had my back to the fullest. She carried me up the mountains one time, with my 60-pound backpack and my McLeod fire tool that weighted another twenty pounds. she was super strong, physically, and mentally. I loved her. If it weren't for her, I wouldn't have made it. My auntie Kamal liked Ashely too. She would feed her on visits when we had the time together.

I was very blessed through my whole prison term. I couldn't believe the people who came out to see me, like my grandma. I remember telling my dad she had come to see me, and he said, "What?!" He couldn't believe it. He told me she must really love me. She didn't even see him, and he had been at a prison close to her house.

I was working my whole time at Fire Camp, but they don't pay inmates real money. But then, I got accepted into a program in San Diego for low-level inmates who have two years or less. You're telling me I get an opportunity to be in San Diego and working making real money? I'm out of Fire Camp! I was tired of that prison money.

My first "real" prison job. I worked at the sewing factory. It was cool learning how to sew with an industrial sewing machine. I did that for about a month, then got promoted to the cutting table. Three inmates at a time were allowed to have that job, and you had to be a certain height. The tables were tall, the space was limited, and you needed space to do the work. I felt good about my position.

I got good with the machinery and cutting the fabric. The cutting machinery was super big and heavy. We would make Nomex gear for the firefighters, khaki clothes for the men at PIP (a psychiatric facility inside of the state's prisons), boxers, and the women's clothing.

I learned a lot working there. I got paid 30 cents an hour when everyone else was at 20 cents unless you were a lifer. They were paid between 50 and 75 cents an hour, and they were done paying off restitution. They got to keep all their money.

Fire Camp pay hadn't been any better. You had to work super hard for that dollar. When you go on fires for an extended period of time, that's when you make your money. I remember going on this fire in Napa Valley that lasted for about a month. It was nasty. Fire was burning down everything.

I had just graduated and was brought to this fire ten days before it was out. It was my first fire experience, and it was crazy. I was at the top of the mountain, cold, scared, not knowing what to do. Thank goodness I had these two friends that I had met from San Diego, Rebecca, and Shelly. We didn't know each other before, but we had mutual friends, come to find out.

They had my back. When it was time to bed down, I thought we would go somewhere and sleep, but they told me no, we sleep right here. Just when I had stopped crying, too.

Rebecca and Shelly let me sleep in the middle of them and told me what to do to keep warm. I was thankful for them. All I could think about was bears, lions, spiders, snakes, bugs… I couldn't sleep.

I saved $1500 going to Fire Camp, so in the end it was beneficial.

Around
April 3, 2015

I get to this next program in San Diego, and I'm so happy. I'm starting to feel a little normal again. We get to wear real clothes, not prison jumpsuits. We had to wear ankle monitors though, because we were allowed to go out and find jobs once we make it to the third phase and graduate a vocational training class.

The training class prepares you to go back into society and teaches you how to conduct yourself in a professional manner on job interviews and with people in general. I thought I already knew all that; I had jobs before. But I ain't gone lie, I didn't know all that I thought I did. I learned good things from that class.

When I arrived at the vocational training program, the first person I called was my dad. I let him know how excited I was to be home. We were on a blackout period for two or three weeks before we could interact with society. You were only allowed one phone call, and mine was to my dad, to tell him all about the program and the benefits I can gain.

All I can remember him saying is, "Don't you come home in a few months?"

I laughed and said, "I wish. I got a little over a year left, Dad."

His responses surprised me. "I hope I make it that long, Lacole."

I said, "What? What you mean?"

He laughed and said, "Girl, I am playing. You know Deana be driving me crazy," and brushed me off.

I don't know if I really believed him. My sister Keyna wasn't really telling me what was going on with my dad while I was in prison, so I really didn't know, but when my auntie Kamal came to see me, she said she had seen my dad and he had gotten skinny. I knew he was a diabetic and alcoholic. I didn't know what else was going on.

My dad wasn't playing. I get to the program April 3, 2015. My dad died in May. I was under the impression I'm coming home to take care of my dad. God had other plans. I was so hurt to hear that news. My heart was in pieces.

God works in mysterious ways. I wasn't supposed to go to the program until months later, but they ended up pulling me earlier than I expected, for whatever reason.

The supervisor of the whole west care foundation happened to know my parents. He grew up with my mom and uncles. When my dad died, I was out of the blackout period, but I had to go through another process to start getting out the house, and that took up to three months.

All the same, I was able to help my grandmother and Auntie Pansy out with a few things that needed to be taking care of for my dad, and they let me attend the funeral under supervision. My counselor at the time took me. She was cool, she didn't invade my privacy, and was respectful of the situation.

The funeral turned out to be a pleasant experience out in society for me, besides the little embarrassment I had on my way up to the alter to read a poem I had written for my dad. I had on a white dress and had bled through, but luckily, I had my auntie Pansy there to help me.

I had not seen family and friends in a while. That was the first time I got to see my niece Maliyah from not behind bars. My sister Trice had come down on leave and brought Maliyah to CIW when she was only three months old. I was sad I had already missed her birth and her baby years after.

I hated that I was only getting to see my family under these circumstances, but it all worked itself out, even the negativity some family members shot my way. I hadn't seen my big cousin Bree in years. This cousin didn't like me growing up. She was the one who told me growing up she hated seeing me come with her dad to her house. Her dad always babysat me.

Bree saw me at the funeral and said, "I'm mad at you. I can't believe you went to prison." I looked at her, smiled and said, "I know," and reached out for a hug. I shook my head to myself and thought, some people.

This isn't the time or the place.

Still to this day, I don't know what really happened to my dad. Deana never reached out to me about anything. In fact, I feel she tries to avoid me so I will never ask her about my father. She always acted like she liked me, but I know she really didn't for whatever reason. I always felt a little jealousy from her.

During this time, my counselor was trying to help me get access to resources and get me to the right person for medical help for my bleeding. The program in San Diego didn't offer Medi-Cal to us, something about us still being in custody, which wasn't quite fair since the same programs in Los Angeles and Bakersfield were giving their girls Medi-Cal. I went down to the county building to try and get Medi-Cal, only to find out I've had it since 2005, which means it never stopped being active.

God is so good! There were about a hundred women in that program, and only a hand full of us had Medi-Cal. All of us from San Diego. I started going back and forth to a doctor my auntie Kamal helped me find.

She had just gone through getting a hysterectomy.

Around June 2015

I go to Sharp Chula Vista Medical Center. I had this Korean doctor, super nice and cute. I suggest a hysterectomy right away. He laughs and tells me to slow down. "Let's see other options we can do to try and fix the problem first," he says. For some reason, I felt the problem couldn't be fixed.

He wants me to think about it for a month. He tells me I'm young with no kids; I might regret it. Then he tells me he can perform a partial hysterectomy and leave my ovaries, so if I decided I do want kids I would still have my eggs. I made up my mind. The bleeding wouldn't stop. It was only getting worse. I'm mentally drained at this point. I almost want to kill myself. "Please," I tell him, "Let's do this."

I start feeling like this was karma from having all those abortions. I go in for surgery on August 2, 2015. I will never forget, my parole officer had to chauffeur me, and she had no sympathy for me at all.

One of my family members was allowed to come to the hospital to support me, but they can't bring me anything. That was the agreement. My auntie Kamal is there.

Before I dose off, I hear the doctor telling the parole officer I can't go into surgery with the ankle monitor on. She needs to take it off. He highly doubts I'll be escaping in surgery or right after surgery.

The parole officer tells my auntie Kamal she can't be there anymore and makes her leave at this point. My auntie was pissed. She didn't trust leaving me there alone with just this officer.

They took my uterus and left my ovaries.

I'm having so much fun being pampered at the hospital regardless of the pain I'm in.

Meanwhile, *the parole officer* is *trying to ruin it for me*. She caused a hazard by trying to plug my ankle monitor in. The nurse wasn't having it. They made her take it off and didn't let her put that back on me until the next day. She made sure to tell the nurses I'm an inmate, I'm not to have visitors, and made them take the phone out of the room.

I get it! Too bad none of that was on my mind. Healing was my only focus, getting better, being able to walk again.

When I finally healed, I felt like Jezebel in the Bible when she touched Jesus' garment and was healed. I felt like a whole new woman. All I can say is, thank you, God, for healing me.

My visits while I was in the program were the best. I was eating everything you can name. Auntie Kamal, Lamya and Jaasau would be there visiting often, and Latrice and Aaliyah even came when they were in town.

I was very blessed. I did not want for nothing. What the devil meant for bad, God turned it all into good! I didn't want to get comfortable at the program. I knew I wasn't coming back to be an inmate ever again. I wasn't about this life. God had made it that easy for me to get through, and now I had to make good.

I get a job at Qualcomm Stadium as a concession stand worker and housekeeper. I would wash the towels and linens for the club, making $15 an hour. It was super cool working there. I would occasionally run into people I know.

I was good to a point, but temptation was killing me. I can't tell you what it really was. My dad being gone, my time being short, my hormones being off the roof. I will never know.

I stop caring. I started drinking, smoking weed. I had a girlfriend at the program and I started bringing her stuff that wasn't allowed.

The program wouldn't phase her up to let her get out and get a job and manage business. She was "stuck inside the house," as we call it, the whole time she was there. She was a hothead from Los Angeles. She would disrespect everybody in that house, from staff to inmates. She didn't care.

At the program, one of the staff monitors, Tony, happened to be the same guy I told you about when I was young. He would come over and get my mom high and have sex with her. What a coincidence. He was still fake and phony in my eyes. When he saw me, he would act so happy and surprised, talking about how he misses my mom, he feels so bad about my dad, blah blah blah.

He assumed Apple was my girlfriend. We never showed it at the program at first. In the program, you weren't allowed to date or do anything that took your focus off yourself. It wasn't acceptable.

I wasn't about to lose working privileges or my ability to leave the house over people saying Apple was my girl. Rumors around the house was I already had a cell phone, which was true

I had gotten a cell phone after I was running late from work one day due to transportation. We weren't allowed to get rides from anyone but staff members. Anytime you're running late, you must call and check in and let someone know.

I'm asking everyone at the trolley station if I could use their phone. There looking at me like, where is yours? I'm telling them the situation, that I'm in a program and can't have a phone, that only made it worse. People really weren't going to let me use their phones after that; they were saying they didn't want to get involved. I didn't want to go through that embarrassment ever again. I got a phone and kept it at work and brought it home on the weekends. I got it for emergencies.

Apple started acting like I'm obligated to bring her stuff. She's feeling me more because of all the stuff I'm doing for her, and she wants to use the phone to call whoever. That's where I messed up. She was also younger than me. Things started getting serious. I played along, knowing I really had no intentions of staying with her. I know I like men but I'm with her because there ain't none around right now and I'm bored. But honestly, after five years, I'm tired of women.

One night, Tony was walking through the halls and caught me in

Apple's room. We were not doing anything, but he made a big deal out of it, wrote me up and everything. I respected it for what it was. This is your job, Mr. Officer. I know you're going to get a bonus at the end of the month. Thanks, Tony.

I'm sure he knows. I'm out there drinking and smoking weed as well.

One night, when I arrive back to the house, Tony looks me in my eyes tells me how pretty I looked, and how I reminded him of my mom.

That was the night I came from a holiday party at Qualcomm Stadium. They let me and a few other girls that worked their attend.

The two other girls and I leave the house together for the party, and things are crazy immediately. I remember it was raining. We get on the bus, on our way to transfer to the trolley. We go into 7-Eleven and get us a Four Loko. We start drinking them as soon as we got them, getting ready for the party.

Rumor was, one of the girls I happen to be with that night does coke when she was outside the house. It happens to be true. She knew I was from San Diego and that I was cool. I was the perfect candidate. She asked if I knew where she can get coke. Of course, I did.

I called the plug, who was a long-time friend. He was already bringing me whatever I needed to my job when I would ask. That's how I got the cell phone. He comes and brings us everything I ask for that night. He's feeling my friend, talking to her, and this whole time my other friend is feeling sick. The alcohol made her start throwing up. Now she sick and doesn't want to go in the party.

I take her up to the trolley seat, sit with her and help her clean herself up, thinking to myself, this isn't good. Please sober up before we get back to the program, otherwise we're all going down.

Meanwhile, my other friend Sandra is high on coke and ready to party. I got one friend ready to party and the other down. I don't know what to do.

My homeboys arrive at the trolley station. They were attending the party too. They took the trolley because they didn't want to risk DUIs. I was shocked to see them. One of my coworkers was a super funny guy.

He looks at my homegirl and says, "Damn, what is up with baby?" She had thrown up on her shirt.

To make a long story short, we end up at the party, eating and dancing and playing raffles. I was happy to get there; I was starving at that point.

On our way back after the party, my friend Sandra felt the night was still young. She wants me to call the connect back to get more drugs before we get back to the program. He comes back, we get another bottle of Hennessy, and we sit at a Starbucks and do us.

Sandra got freaky off coke. She licked me in the mouth and told me to lick the coke off my hand. I acted like I did, but I didn't. She was cute too. I didn't mind the attention if Apple didn't find out. I didn't want Apple trying to fight her or anything because I wasn't tripping it didn't make me any difference I wasn't scared of Apple.

When I get back to the program, Apple accuses me of being out with dudes. I told her I was out with Sandra and Lauren. Little did she know if you know what I mean.

Not to long after that, my parole officer started acting weird, she would ask me to test randomly. I tried turning in someone else's urine, but she caught me. She's never looked in the stall before. Why this time, suddenly? I'm thinking to myself, somebody got to be telling but whatever — I knew I was doing wrong. She knew it too. Back to prison I go.

The only thing that sucked about that was. I was about to start a training program at Kitchens for Good, a culinary arts school that offers classes to felons for free. I always wanted to be a high dining chef. I messed up that opportunity, trying to get faded. I felt bad about that.

I was thankful I didn't catch more time for the drugs, and that they never found the cell phone. That automatically would have been an extra 90 days.

Around March 20, 2017

I went back to prison, with eight months to go. Apple came back with me. She stated that I was her best friend and that I'm the reason she makes it through the program every day. If I leave, she leaves.

I know the people running the program were thinking to themselves, they should have gotten rid of me a long time ago if that's all it took to get rid of her. None of the staff liked her. They were happy to see her go for sure.

We went to a prison in Bakersfield call McFarland. The set-up was new to us. It was dorm living, with over a hundred girls. It sucked. It was dirty and nasty but had I messed up and now I had to suffer the consequences.

Before making it to McFarland, we had to stop at CIW first for a month, to wait to get endorsed to go to McFarland. I left before Apple. When I get to McFarland, I met this cool girl from San Diego name Peace. We grew up in the same neighborhood but had never crossed paths, probably because she had been in prison already for six years when I met her. She was younger than me and sweet as pie. She would braid my hair and cook for us. We became close and we still talk today.

While I was at McFarland, I'm starting to think about who I can live with when I get out. I can't go anywhere. I'm going to be on parole, and I don't want to mess up. It's bad enough I had already been sent back to prison. I was embarrassed to tell my sisters.

I reached out to my cousin Badr and auntie La Belle. I knew they had the space available. In their house, it was my cousin, her son, and one of my other cousins. It would have been the perfect place for me. Everyone that was around there was a positive influence. That's what I needed to surround myself with so I can stay on the right track when I get home.

Unfortunately, they had to reject me due to family business. I was hurt. I had thought they would give me a chance and the opportunity to get on my feet.

I wait a few more weeks before I even started to think of anyone else to reach out to. Then, the perfect person comes to mind: Jaasau. She's a diligent Christian lady who takes care of her kids. She and her man are on a break right now, so there might be room for me at hers.

I also had to take into consideration the fact that I am going to be on parole. This is a big responsibility for someone, to let me come to their house with their kids.

I give it a shot. I reach out to Jaasau and make sure to run down my rules and regulations with her. She's all for it. she has always been a good friend, even when we did have our falling outs.

I find out the prison is giving milestones to 85% now, which wasn't offered to me when I first started my sentence. The program didn't give you any time off; they felt you were already in society working, so you had to finish all your time up in the program.

So, from here, I could try to get back into the program and work, or I could try to make it home early. I start thinking wanting to go home earlier was better than working. The faster your home, the faster you can start your life over. It worked out for me. I didn't question God's plan.

I take a computer and criminal thinking class. I stayed busy to try and make my time go by. The only thing was I really didn't like at McFarland was their church. When I was out of prison at the program, I had found a good one I was attending, called Linda Vista Baptist in Kearny Mesa. I would go with my good friend Leslie, whom I had met at CIW and who was an usher in the church. We ended up getting close at the program. We would go to church together with a few of the other ladies in the house.

Apple goes home before me. She ends up going home early after taking classes to get milestones as well. It was a bittersweet feeling. That was my girl. We were together every day when we weren't in classes. I was happy to see her go; all that meant was that I was next.

We talked on the phone often after she left. She sent me my last food box and money order. She stuck to her word.

Around October 17, 2017

"Colbert, roll up, you're going home." I was already up. The police let you wake up an hour earlier on your released date, so you can get ready with no interruptions. The girls were trying to give me hugs and say their goodbyes. Not to be rude, but I don't have time for this. This is the reason I'd said my goodbyes last night before I went to sleep. I was ready to go home to my family.

I get to receiving in no time. They give me my Adidas outfit, my shoes, my ID that my sister and Lamya had bought for me, and my check that I came with for three thousand dollars. I was out.

They drove me and another girl that was from San Diego to the Grey Hound station and sent us on our way.

*T*hat was my first time riding the Grey Hound. I didn't want my sister and Lamya driving the full six hours to pick me up, plus they had my two-year-old niece with them. I decided to take the grey hound to Los Angeles to Apple's house, which was two hours away from San Diego.

Apple and her mom picked me up *from the station.* We grab a bite to eat and *then* went back to her house. *That was* my first time seeing some real housing projects. They made our ghetto look nice. Now I see how Los Angeles girls can be real thugs. San Diego ain't got nothing on them.

I wasn't there for long, *half an hour, before* Lakeyna and Lamya arrive.

They pull up and I'm so happy. We're all screaming, smiling, hugging, and kissing.

Finally, it takes us about one hour and 45 minutes to get back to San Diego. We go straight to the parole office, which was a waste of time. They weren't expecting me until the next morning.

Lamya couldn't wait to roll up some weed and get me high. That was the only drug you can really do on parole because they didn't test for marijuana, for some reason. I hear rumors that it's too expensive for them to test us for that. I hit it one time and I'm high as a kite. I can't stop laughing, on top of the fact that I'm already silly.

We go to my favorite place for dinner, Red Lobster. It hasn't changed a bit from what I remember. I order a Bahama Mama and ultimate feast. I'm in heaven. It feels so good to be free.

We go to Auntie Kamal's after that. They want to see me and everybody is showing me love.

The following weekend, Auntie Kamal throws me a party. She loves doing it big. I was surprised to see Auntie La Belle pull up on her motorcycle. I heard she had beat cancer. I was so happy to see her. I was over the fact she rejected me. Growing up, I always admired her and wished I were her daughter. She was an incredibly beautiful lady and a firefighter and would let me ride with her on the fire truck in the Martin Luther King Day parades back in the day. Her house was nice. Visiting her was the only time I ever got McDonald's. She had gotten married to a police officer who was a nice guy, but after that I really didn't see her anymore, until my mom's funeral. She gave me $1000 to help with the service. I was so happy to see her at my party, and she let me know if I needed anything to reach out. She knew I was fresh out of prison with nothing.

It was a lovely day with food, drinks, music, you name it, and lots of family love. I was shocked to see some of the faces that showed up that day, some I hadn't seen in years, probably since high school. It was surprising and very touching. I really enjoyed myself. Apple even made it. I enjoyed everyone's company and being free.

When I got home, I didn't go straight to Jaasau's house. I spend the first week at Auntie Kamal's, which turned out to be a blessing. During that first week, I heard my cousin's friend Nipsey, who had worked with me at the stadium, had a car for sale. It was his baby's mama's car; she didn't want it anymore and was trying to get a new one.

It was a nice Toyota Altima, champagne color, clean inside and out. They had taken particularly good care of it. He was selling it for four thousand but ended up giving it to me for three thousand. I was so thankful; it was well worth the four.

My second week home, I finally make it to Jaasau's. Her home was nice, and she made me feel at home immediately. She let me stay in her daughters' room during the time I was there. I felt bad. I didn't have anything to give her for letting me stay. I went down to get an EBT card so I could at least offer her food while I was there. I made sure I kept her house clean for her and the kids. I would cook and babysit whenever she needed. She would make jokes and say I'm the perfect house cleaner. I was happy to try and help her out. It was nothing, compared to what she was doing for me.

I would wake up every morning at 7am, eat, shower and make sure I was on that computer when Jaasau and the kids left. I was job searching from 8am to 5pm. I made looking for a job a job within itself. It would get discouraging at times. It seemed like no one hires felons, even though in those vocational training classes in prison they tell you companies get paid to hire felons through a system called bonding.

There is an UPS seasonal job fair happening at the Metro center. The online listing said to be there on Wednesday at 1:30 for further instructions. I was there at 1:15, dressed to impressed, telling myself, I'm not leaving here without this job. I'm tired of looking I need a job now so I can get back on my feet. I'm not used to living with anyone.

People showed up. I'm not intimidated. May the best person win today. We all go in sit down to listen to a speech, then wait to be called. I get called by this lady named Jessica. I will never forget that interview. We both introduced ourselves and then she starts asking me questions. I'm on it, answering all the interview questions on point. I'm feeling great, confident.

After she was done with the questions, just before the end of my interview, something comes over me. I don't know what made me say it, but I looked her dead in the eyes and said, "Look, Jessica, I just got released from prison three weeks ago. Since then, I've moved on, paid my debt to society. I'm truly forever remorseful. Being in prison refined my ability to be a team player and leader when necessary. I will not let you down. Please, give me a chance. I will be an asset to this company."

She looked at me her expression unreadable. She said, "What were you in for?"

I told her; second degree robbery use of a firearm. She cringes slightly, as if to say "ouch," then begins looking over my resume.

She said, "You went to Fire Camp." Her tone was almost impressed. "You can handle this job." "Sure can, with no problems," I said.

She smiled and spoke. "Ok, Lacole, I'll be in touch.

I left the job fair, not knowing if I really believed her.

The following week, I had to go to the parole office and test. The officer asks me how's job searching going. I bust out in tears and tell him how I've been job searching nonstop, but no one is calling me back. How I had an interview with UPS last week, and still nothing. He tells me that UPS won't hire me. He had or has a friend who works there. They get paid well and get good benefits, but my charges will probably affect me. At the end, he gives me this paper with resources on it and tells me to look there and not to give up.

I grab the paper, rolling my eyes, and leave.

Let me tell you how God works. I get in my car, drive for two minutes and my phone rings. It's Jessica, letting me know I got the job with UPS. She tells me where to be the next morning along with further details.

I had just stopped crying, and now I'm crying and screaming all over again full of joy. I can't believe it! I called that parole officer so fast and told him the good news. He couldn't even believe it. He had just said that

UPS wasn't going to hire me. All the same, he was happy for me. You can't stop God's work.

Meantime between time, Apple and I are *still talking.* She would come down *from Los Angeles sometimes to hang out* and I *would show her a good time clubbing* in San Diego. I would drive to Los Angeles to see her too.

It all *got old* quick. *I was over it, especially when she had gone back to jail on a violation.* She started lying too much for me. I'm thinking, it wasn't that serious. You live up there, I live down here. Do you, boo. I'm not made for a woman anyway. I ain't waking up to the same thing as me; I need a man. It was fun while it lasted.

Now I'm single and ready to mingle, right? Nope — I'm just playing. I really want to take this time and work and make money so I can try and be out of Jaasau's within the next six months.

It took time to get used to working at UPS. The hours were crazy: the 1:00am to 9:00am graveyard shift wasn't no joke, and it wasn't a guarantee they were going to keep you once you were hired. You had to go through a three-month probation period before they hire you permanently. I had to work my behind off those first three months to really prove myself. But the hard work pays off. Three months later, I'm permanent.

My auntie Le Belle had told me if I needed anything to let her know, so one day I reach out. I can really use a laptop to manage my business and start writing my book. Tooper had inspired me to share my story after I'd told him a bit about my past. Then I start thinking to myself about how when I was in prison sitting behind those brick walls, I wanted so badly to be a youth mentor. I felt I had learned a lot, had a lot of wise and encouraging advice to share with those who may be struggling or feeling stuck in the horrible lifestyle I once lived.

So, I ask Auntie Le Belle if she can help with a laptop to get this project started. She says she can't help me with anything. Absolutely nothing. Everything was a no.

I totally understand; God will provide.

Life is good. I'm on the right track, going to church. I started going back to Linda Vista Church. I never became a member, but I always wanted to join their choir.

I give myself a pat on the back. I've been out a little over a month and now I'm working with a car, thinking about how to make legit money. I don't have a criminal thought on my mind. All I know is, I ain't never going back to prison. I won't even spit on the sidewalk.

Now that I'm out, I see that my dad was right: nothing has changed. My dad told me from experience that when I came home, everything was going to be the same. I wasn't missing out on anything. It was so true. Same people, same clubs, just a different day.

In fact, I wish I would have come home and met new people, instead of feeling like I was moving backwards. That would have saved me a lot of unnecessary drama. I'm thinking, I'm coming home, trying to repair friendships, when deep down inside, these people are mad at me for whatever reason.

If I'm not with Jaasau in my free time, I'm with Lamya, hanging out catching up. I had missed my bestie. While in prison, I had expressed to her that if I ever was a bad friend to her, I apologize and I want to do better as a person this time around. We had been friends since we were kids. We have been through a lot.

Prison made me realize that friends are important. The fact that she was there for me after the two years I was in, that really touched me. Honestly, she didn't ever have to reach out to me. Prior into going into prison, we were rocky.

While I was in prison, she tells me about a new drug she's trying. It's the same drug I've always wanted to try, but I never have because I'm not too fond of nosebleeds or white drugs. In the past, around friends, I had seen this drug cause nosebleeds, and that was the only thing that had stopped me from trying it. (Lamya can't do drugs anymore for several reasons.)

I knew when I came home, I wanted to behave differently. But I felt like to hang out and have fun, I had to be able to relate with everyone else on drugs.

Around January 2018

One night, my homeboy is having a going away party. We're all partying hard that night, I end up trying it, this drug. I didn't feel anything at first. They made me do more until I did. All I can say is, I couldn't go to sleep.

Tooper arrives shortly after us. Tooper is my homeboy from back in the day. I met him and his brother through Lamya; they're all from the same territory. They were some of the bests around back then.

When I met Tooper for the first time, I remember thinking he was attractive. There was something about his eyes and eyelashes that I loved. I always preferred dark dudes, but these guys were pimps and I wasn't hoeing. I would rob you if anything.

Lamya was feeling Tooper's brother Raanan. When they would call Lamya to kick it, we would get happy and call them our babies and go kick it with them.

They didn't have a clue we were feeling like this either. That was the best part. We would always play our cards right. We knew we wanted to kick it and they looked at us like homegirls. They always had the top shelf drink and smoke. They lived nice, and it was cool to be in their company. We would be living it up when we were around them.

Tooper and I end up building our own relationship outside of Lamya. I lived on Willie James Jones on Imperial. He would come over when he was in the hood. We would go to this hole-in-the-wall breakfast spot called Eileen's that was a few blocks away from my house. That was our spot. We would chill in the bed and watch T.V.

Other than that, we would smoke and drink and lay in the bed watching television. We never had an intimate relationship. I don't really know why. I remember one night when he came over, I was fresh out the shower. Normally, I would run and hurry to go put on clothes, but that night I stayed in my robe. He didn't bite. That only made me want him more, but still, we never got to it.

He ends up going to prison a few years before me, sentenced to five years. He tried reaching out while in prison, but I wasn't feeling him. I'm not into prison guys. I ain't got time to be putting my money on books and driving hours away for visits, With global Tel link on my phone. That's out. I ain't got the patience for that. He didn't know I had my own issues going on at the time too.

While I was in prison, he started dating one of Lamya's friends, Kira, *who* was my play brother Reg's little sister. *H*er brother *and I were* best friends *from* middle school all the way up until he was killed. She was younger than us *and* I never buil*t* a relationship with her. I'd see her in passing, she*'d* see me, we'd *talk a bit,* keep it pushing, if that. Kira and Tooper end up breaking up on my way home from prison.

I say that to say this: that was my first time seeing Tooper in years. I had talked to him one day when he was at Lamya's when I called. Other than that, between his prison time and mine, we'd lost touch. It was so good to see him now. He had cut his hair. I liked the look. He had braids when he went away. He walked in, spotted me, and we both started smiling from ear to ear. He came straight to me and gave me a warm hug.

I was thinking to myself, you can get it. We've still got unfinished business we can handle with yo sexy self. I went home to tell Jaasau what was up with me and Tooper, how I had seen him at the party. Jaasau is also a mutual friend of Kira's.

Around February 2018

Tooper and I go to breakfast, just like old times. I'm not really trying to get too serious with him. I might want to have a little bit of fun, but I didn't want to be in a relationship right now. I wanted to stay single for a while. And he's in the process of breaking up with someone. He lives in his apartment, she lives in hers, but they're still seeing each other from time to time. I know it was an issue when I posted a picture of us on Facebook of our first date and somebody took a screenshot of it and supposedly sent it to her. It was a cute date downtown, we rode the set of love, he bought me a rose, and we partied.

He needed to straighten that up. I wasn't seeing anyone else, and honestly, I really didn't plan on this to even happen. I always loved Tooper as a person, but I really didn't want to date anyone out of southeast because you can never have them to yourself. There's always some type of connection to a person or place or thing that you want to leave in the past and move forward, except you can't.

One day led to another. We were really enjoying each other's company. He's sweet. We finally do have sex, and it was enjoyable. At least I can use him for that, if nothing else, I thought. I am fresh out and haven't been around man in a long time.

I started staying over Tooper's a lot. I would go to Jaasau's, change my clothes and grab some extras while I was there, and then leave again. When we see each other, Jaasau would ask me questions about Tooper. I told her everything, then she wanted to know if we had sex. I told her yes, and she asked how it was. I told her it was good and smiled.

Apparently, Jaasau had heard different reviews. She told me no, it's not good, and I've probably had better. I probably enjoyed it because I was fresh out of prison. Ouch. Okay, you know what feels good to my vagina. I kept those thoughts to myself, never wanting to disrespect her.

Jaasau also had me feeling like I owed Kira an explanation when that wasn't even who Tooper had been dating last. I gave into that though, just so everyone could be happy.

Honestly, I don't think I was ever Kira's favorite. When I got out, Lamya asked her to do my hair for my party. *Her reply was that* she didn't feel comfortable doing it the way I wanted it for free. I wanted tracks added in between my real hair. My real hair was a nice length, but it was thin. I wanted to make it look fuller. She said she would do it in a ponytail, how she wanted to do it.

I don't know if Lamya was trying to get it done for free. She knew I was fresh out with nothing, and I guess she didn't have the money to spot me.

Lamya was living with this girl *when I got out of prison and, prior to that, her house was* being *renovated. I remember Lamya inviting me over to her house.* When I get there, Lamya calls Kira to let her know I was there. She asked Lamya to go outside with me. She didn't want me in her house, basically. I wish Lamya would have let her know before I came. I told Lamya, "It's all good, you don't have to come outside. I'll leave." And that's exactly what I did.

I move in with Tooper after three months. This end up working out great, since Jaasau and her man were working things out around this time and he was moving in.

I don't know what happened then. Things started getting super messy with me dating Tooper. I don't know if it was Jaasau or Lamya, but they were both blaming each other. At that point, I didn't even care. I'm not in high school anymore, and everybody needs to mind their own business.

I'm not asking anyone about their relationships. I don't care who's sleeping with whom.

That was one thing I realized when I came home after being away for many years. My time in prison gave me a chance to reflect on my life. I knew I wanted different than I was taught. And I'm the only one who can do that for myself. With that being said, I must change my ways of thinking and how I speak from the start.

I guess me speaking up for myself made Jaasau and I go our separate ways. I'm sure she got tired of her name always being in the mix when there was drama going on between me and Lamya. We had been going through this since high school. Honestly, I'm tired of the nonsense myself were too old for this.

I will always love and respect Jaasau as a person *and* I will forever appreciate what she did for me. God puts everyone in your life for a reason. She was there for me when my own family wasn't. That's something I'll never forget. I will forever wish her and her family the best in life. Blessings to you, Jaasau.

I feel like when you're down and out, when people feel like you need them, they like you better that way than when you're getting on your feet, doing it for yourself. Being that help and hand to someone else gives so many people the validation they desire.

When God takes people out my life, I don't question it, if I know in my heart, I didn't do anything wrong this time. If I can honestly say that, then I must move on with my life. You can't go through life living by how the world views you, because most people's view of you is never going to include you changing. These types of people don't even see change for themselves.

All that living up to others' expectations is going to do is continuously make you try and prove yourself. I did that all my life. Now, I don't need validation from anyone today to make me feel like I'm somebody. That's what I have God for.

What do I have to prove to anyone, and for what? Ain't none of these people doing nothing for me. Honestly, no one is doing better than the next person. Everybody is faking it until they make it, and we're all just standing still.

The people that I grew up with — and grew up to be like —are all a certain way. These people have never had a decent job. They don't know how to start an emergency fund to save up. They're not thinking about working, if they ain't thinking about school. They look forward to continuing relying on the county, getting EBT and aid. They think this is normal, just thinking all wrong, about how to go steal and fraud, and not caring that their children are seeing all this.

I grew up inheriting the generational curses. Nobody is married for the right reasons, most are committing adultery or just marrying to see what they can get. You can't trust a soul. Your friends are in competition with you and you don't even know. All you hear and all you think is, I got to catch up. Catch up to what? At least make it make sense. Nobody out here owns anything or has their kids doing anything productive.

I'm not talking about dressing them up in their best outfits, making sure they look good for social media. *Most of the time, they're struggling with something else anyway.* All I'm trying to say is, nothing is done out of love.

I was wasting my time trying to impress these individuals.

I had to look in the mirror and ask myself, what is wrong with you, Lacole? You're beating yourself up over this.

Live for God, someone who genuinely loves you. He will never leave you nor forsake you.

People will do what you allow them to do. I've been mentally abused my whole life. One thing I asked God to enable me to do before I was released was to stand firm. I wanted to have my NO mean NO, and my YES mean YES. I'm able to do just that today. I know that when people do things for you, they tend to think they can talk to you or treat you any kind of way because they're doing you a favor. To that, I say NO. Treat people how you want to be treated.

Shortly after I move in with Tooper, he gets hit at work by a OnTrac delivery truck. He's out of work. Then, he finds out his dad has pancreatic cancer. I'm trying to support him the best way I know how. I don't have my parents anymore; I know the feeling.

When I met his dad, he wasn't as sick yet. He was still up and active. He reminded me of my dad. A few months later, he was on hospice and we had moved in his apartment to take care of him. It was perfect timing for Tooper being off work.

It was four of us taking care of his dad: Me, Tooper, his brother Raanan, and Raanan's girlfriend. I swear sometimes, it felt like it was just me, and all this on top of going to work the graveyard shift at UPS.

I would leave and come home to everyone asleep. I would have to give Tooper's dad his medicine, then try and feed him. It got to the point that I was the only one changing his diaper, asides from the nurses who came to check on him occasionally. That was a big responsibility for someone who hadn't been out of prison a full six months and was trying to work and get on her feet.

And yet, somehow, caring for him was special. For some reason, when I was taking care of Tooper's dad, it felt like I was taking care of my own dad. I never got the chance to be there for him when he passed, and this felt like me making it up to him somehow. It was weird. I can't describe the feeling; only God knows.

Around
May 22, 2018

Tooper's dad died about ten days later, while I was changing him. I couldn't believe this man, whom I didn't even really know, died in my arms. Just like that, I thought, it was over.

Our addiction picked up after that. Tooper took it hard and wasn't working due to the accident. School was on break for him too. He had lots of time on his hands and a lot on his mind, and he turned to drugs to try and numb the pain. I knew just how he felt. I would try to give him his space. At times, you end up taking your emotions out on the people closest to you. I tried to be understanding.

Tooper's dad left money behind for his boys, and a nice amount. They were shocked. However, when drugs are involved, things can get ugly. Everyone wants their cut.

In the aftermath, Tooper wants to keep his dad's car, the black Lexus. Technically the car is half his and half his brother's, so he must give his brother Raanan money for it. Raanan is running things.

The funeral is in May and his dad's affairs are settled not long after. By June, Tooper finds time to clear his mind.

Around June 16, 2018

"We're going to lunch at 1:30," Tooper tells me this morning. "Be ready and look nice. We're going to thank Ms. Young for helping us with my dad. Your sister is coming to." Ms. Young had been a friend of his dad's and had safekept his money after he died. Sorting out his dad's affairs was Tooper's first time meeting her, but she had done his family a favor, issuing out all the funds.

"That's nice. Okay, I'll be ready," I say, not thinking anything of it.

We arrive at the restaurant and Ms. Young and Tooper's play sister Lahja is there, sitting at the table. I love Lahja. She had also reached out to me while in prison. It's always good to see her and she's always full of positive energy. She was one of me and Tooper's mutual friends whom I grew up with. Tooper and Lahja were older than me and Lamya, but we all grew up together.

Shortly after that, Raanan and his girlfriend join us too. Everyone is ordering food and drinks, having an enjoyable time.

Then, suddenly, Tooper stands me up, gets on one knee, and asks me to marry him. I couldn't believe it. When did he find the time to get this beautiful ring?

I was so surprised; my body felt like it was going into shock. I held my face and started to cry and said, "Yes, I'll marry you." I knew that I loved Tooper, and that he was a good man. Sure, he had things he needed to

Healed

deal with on his own, and I didn't know if I were ready for it, but I knew I would pray my way through.

Jealousy and envy toward me were turned on high after that. I get it. I'm out and I have a car, a respectable job, and a fiancé. It's God's plan, not mine. I ain't tripping. I have a wedding to plan.

Tooper had given me his dad's Lexus and told me to sell my car. I sold it to Lamya's mom, Ms. Wadud. I sold it to her for extraordinarily little, as a favor. I could have made more money, but I thought of her since her car wasn't that reliable. Plus, I love that lady, and she felt so blessed to have the car. She really appreciated it. She stated that was the nicest car she ever had and she had dreamed about it. That made me feel so good.

Tooper and I are engaged and trying to be happy as can be, but I don't know what was up with Raanan and his girl. We had gotten off to a good start and were even becoming friends. Then, things got ugly. It got to the point to where me and Raanan's girl had words, she said she would expose me for whatever reason and what is there to expose?

I was irritated after that. She had told Tooper that I was trying to get with her friend one night riding to Raanan's album release party. Trying to start drama. Which was not true, soon as her friend met me, she said your pretty, and I thought she was too.

I let Raanan's girl no to meet me at the park, so we can talk out our difference or fight.

I'm assuming she would be used to running things until I came along. I wasn't about to let her run my program. Things had to change. I had gotten tired of her and Raanan trying to run Tooper's life. That caused plenty of tension between the brothers. I'm thinking, you run each other's lives — that's what you're there for. Leave me and my fiancé alone. I got this.

Raanan was super needy by nature. He would call Tooper to do everything for him and Tooper would be right there at his beck and call. If it was ever the other way around, with Tooper asking Raanan for help, Raanan immediately turned negative. He would always bring up the past and what he did for Tooper and how he felt Tooper owed him for that.

That also caused tension between me and Tooper. Raanan would be disrespectful to me. He would call me out by name, say things like I'm weak and broke, and why does his brother want me. All because I'm not letting him run my life, and he feels I'm trying to stop Tooper from doing things for him. I'm fresh out of prison, you're right. All the haters give me a chance to get back on my feet, and then we'll see. I did lose everything I had, and I'm ok with that.

It got to the point that Raanan was trying to take the Lexus back, telling Tooper he needed to give him more money. How am I supposed to get to work? And it's not only me — Tooper's son moved in with us during all this too.

He had just graduated high school. I had gotten him a job with UPS, so now both of us needed the car to get to work. They did not want me to put that car in my name, and I don't understand why. Why are you guys hating? You have cars. I'm trying to get to work, that's it. But Tooper didn't know how to control Raanan or how to set boundaries for his brother, and that hindered Tooper and my relationship. He and his brother had always been close. I guess this is what they were used to.

I got to the point that I didn't care anymore. I was tired of all of them. I was ready to move on without Tooper and his disrespectful family. I don't deserve this. Had they all forgotten who had just taken care of their dying father?

The only reason I stayed around, besides God, was that I knew Tooper was a good guy. He always seemed like he didn't fit in with the bad guys. He was just following them; is how I saw it. Prison had changed him as well. He didn't want to be that same person he went in as when he came home.

He simply didn't have the right influences in his life to lead him in the right direction. The game will suck you dry if you let it. I knew he needed a real good woman in his life. Tooper and I have similar stories, but that's a whole another story.

While Tooper was in prison he would teach his cellmates. He's well-spoken and he reads a lot. He was also learning Spanish. He also taught me a lot. He's one of the people who inspired me to write a book.

Honestly, I never thought I could author of a book. I always hated school, and English was my worse subject. I didn't know how to receive information and collect it. I was never educated enough to even try and pursue anything. I always had dreams, but I never thought they would come true. Jean Michel Basquiat says, "It's not who you are that holds you back, it's who you think you're not."

Today my God has enabled me to become the woman that I thought I would never be. I know how to comprehend information and how to receive it. Now, I know how to collect knowledge. I know how to use big words, how to hold an intelligent conversation, and how to understand it 100% better. I knew I wasn't perfect, but God showed me the way.

Tooper had potential. He was going to school to be an electrician. He was learning and practicing while working. I knew he was going through tough times plus fighting his demons.

I was thinking to myself, do I have the time, energy, and patience to try and help mold this grown man? Is it even possible, or should I say forget it and move on? We ain't married yet.

I go to lunch with Lamya and Maeva to this sushi place one day. I had to confess to Lamya and let her know that what I was saying in prison wasn't just prison talk; I really loved her and wanting our friendship to be better this time.

And I felt like it probably could be better, especially now that Jaasau and I aren't friends anymore. I can give her my all, and now there won't be any games of "who said what," with no more Jaasau in the picture. Jaasau used to tell me how Lamya isn't my friend, how she talks about me and how she says we're not good friends.

Everyone was telling me I shouldn't trust Lamya. She was way too close to Kira, Tooper's ex-girlfriend. I didn't pay it any attention. This is my best friend. I've known her longer than anyone. I had even expressed to Dada how I love Lamya and how I think our friendship was getting much stronger. She was happy to hear that, as she knew we had been through a lot, especially lately.

Tooper and I are getting back on the right track. He defends me

Around June 16, 2018

and has my back like a fiancé should. God tells me he's worth taking a chance on.

I find a venue for our wedding *at Coronado Cays Yacht Club, which is perfect* because *Tooper loves the water. We* wanted to *set the date for November 4, 2019*, the same day as *my dad's birthday*. Deciding on a date turned out to be difficult though. Tooper asked me if I wanted a summer wedding. It didn't sound like a bad idea, especially since we are getting married on the beach in Coronado.

My auntie Kamal had my back to the fullest, helping with all the wedding planning, even though she was stressing me out at times. God bless her soul; she didn't mean no harm. She wanted that day to be special for me, just like I did.

Lamya and I are still good, and our new friendship is still growing stronger. We are planning, getting ready for the big day. Auntie Kamal and the girls are throwing parties, booking party buses, going to wineries and dinners. We're having fun, really enjoying each other's company.

Wedding planning is a ton of work though, and I wish I would have done my research on bridesmaids and maids of honors, and matrons of honor beforehand. I didn't know what a matron of honor was until my cousin Dada told me.

I had chosen my sisters Latrice and Lakeyna from the start to be my maids of honor. I wanted them both near me. Once Latrice couldn't make it due to work, it was just Lakeyna. But she wasn't helping or participating, and I start feeling like she wasn't interested. She was with her friends turning up, like that was more important than my wedding. I start turning my head on her and looking elsewhere.

I start thinking Maeva would be a perfect fit for the job. She was supporting me I grew up with her and look at her like a sister. She's married, she's a good fit. I ran it by her, but she says she didn't want to offend her sister, which is understandable. That is my best friend, after all.

The reason I didn't ask Lamya was because I was going through so many mixed feelings about how she was so close to this girl, Tooper's ex, who didn't like me. I don't know if I truly trusted her when she was around this girl.

I don't know what was being said, but it got back to me that this girl was talking mess, and in front of Lamya. Lamya didn't say anything though, and she didn't tell me.

I knew for a fact what was being told to me was true. This girl just doesn't just talk to be talking. She has never been in the middle of me and Lamya. She was way too young, and I looked at her like a little cousin.

It didn't help, hearing everyone tell me not to trust her and that she's not on my side.

Then I start thinking my cousin Dada was a good fit. I wanted the lineup of my wedding party to stay the same. It had already been messed up due to people tripping, and I didn't want any more feelings to be hurt. This wedding is supposed to be about me and Tooper, and I want things how I want them. It's fair to say, this is my wedding, and I was simply happy they were all in it. I loved them all. On the day of the wedding, I won't care who is what. Please just keep the line up the same and look pretty.

The drama wasn't just over my bridesmaids either. One of Tooper's groomsmen was acting like he didn't want to be in the wedding. For whatever reason, he wasn't giving Tooper straight up answers. He just wouldn't go get fitted.

Rumor later was his baby mama didn't want him walking down the aisle with anyone except Lamya or Maeva. They were all friends from the same territory.

I had the line up the way I wanted it. That's how it was staying. So, we need a replacement groomsman. I feel like people were trying to sabotage my wedding at this point with their childish rivalries. Grow up.

Then the baby mama had the nerve to think it was okay to remain on the guest list, like it's okay to show up without him being in the wedding.

It was beyond immature. He didn't simply tell us from the start that he didn't want to be in the wedding, he just wasn't participating. Meanwhile, Tooper's thinking this was one of his closest homeboys. I would never have thought he would have had problems like this from his so-called homies. People can be coldhearted. That really hurt Tooper.

God works it out like always, and we get a groomsman with no problem. Everything was perfect. I feel he should have been chosen from the start and all these problems could have been avoided.

All this time, Lamya ain't feeling me. She's hearing that I'm talking about her. I'd apparently shared something she told me in confidence with another one of her homegirls, who I thought she trusted, but I don't understand what the big deal is. It was a silly thing, about a cell phone Tooper had in Kira's name from when they were together, and I had shared it with a girl whom Lamya supposedly trusted. Needless to say, things were rough between us for a while.

I guess to remain in the wedding, she stated she had never been in a wedding before and she was excited. Her and Maeva are playing it cool, but they both know something is up. When will we escape the turmoil?

Around August 8, 2019

It was such a beautiful surprise to see my uncle Lagina, my dad's little brother, walk into the bride's rooms as my friend Less was getting me ready for my big day. Less did my hair prior to me going to prison, and we'd become close. I would go the shop every Friday, get my hair done and mix all different kinds of good drinks for us. We'd just chill together and enjoy each other's time. I met a lot of good women there in the shop. One in particular, Wala even reached out to me when I went to prison. I didn't know she even cared for me that much, and hearing from her touched my heart.

I cried soon as I seen my uncle Lagina. He looked just like my dad. He showed up at the perfect time. The original plan was for my brother to walk with me down the aisle. Uncle Lagina ends up walking me, and my brother was behind me holding my veil. I barely made it to the altar before my husband eagerly took me out my uncle's hands. My husband was turned up at the altar. It made me happy and proud that he was ready to marry me, after all we had been through.

Even though things were rocky between our guests, everyone played it cool and the ceremony turned out to be beautiful.

I was only irritated that I really wanted to get good pictures with my wedding party, but only a few hung around. Everybody else had made a beeline for to the alcohol and were fast getting faded. But I made the best of it and worked with what I had.

The wedding reception was cool, for the most part. I was happy my grandma and my auntie Pansy came down. I wasn't sure if people were going to be able to make it, as our wedding was on a Thursday. We knew it might conflict with people's schedules, but still we wished for the best.

Other parts of the wedding were weird. There were certain individuals at my wedding who didn't even acknowledge me, didn't congratulate me, give me a hug, a gift or anything. All I could do was laugh.

You know how uncontrollable black folks could be on account of the alcohol and drugs. Stuff started getting out of control, so I had to cut the wedding short. I told everyone it was time to go. I didn't want anything to happen that would keep me from getting my two-thousand-dollar deposit back.

My husband even got drunk at our wedding and started acting up, going off on my sister's best friend Lina, thinking she had hurt me because she didn't end up being in the wedding. She was supposed to replace Latrice, but we had difficulties with her dress. It didn't come on time. Tooper didn't even know why Lina didn't end up being in the wedding. He just made a wrong assumption, and when he saw her, he wanted to know why she still attended the wedding if she wasn't in it. I think taking it out on her that I made the decision for him about his groomsmen that hurt his feelings.

Everything worked itself out, and I got my deposit back.

Our married life together started out stressful. At that point in time, we were living with my sister in Southeast, trying to save up money and get ourselves together.

Around September 2019

Times can be tough, but God is amazing all the time. After months of hard work, I got a promotion that took me to Phoenix, Arizona.

I was promoted to be a driver. It was a huge upgrade from my previous position. Finally, I'm about to start making real money. I must go for a week very intense training school. It felt like boot camp. But I passed, and now I'm certified to be a UPS driver. I'm super excited for my new journey!

God is working in my favor. I get a call from my parole officer on October 3, saying I'm off parole. They were letting me off parole a year earlier than I was supposed to get off. He tells me to keep up the good work and keep moving forward.

I was so excited. I threw me a bowling party at the Clairemont Bowling Center. I love to bowl, and I had so much to celebrate. I was grateful for the ones that came out and supported that special day with me.

Lamya did show up though, and it seems like the wedding drama still hasn't passed. I'm not aware of the negativity she continued to harbor against me, but apparently, she'd heard that I'm calling her names and saying all sorts of things, and she's believing it. In fact, it's the opposite! No one is telling her all the good things I'm saying.

A month passes and the holiday season is coming up. Lamya lets me know what she's doing for her birthday. I'm not feeling it. I let her know her friends aren't my friends and suggest that we can spend time together on my birthday, which is the next day. She tells me OK, but knowing she has other plans already.

I don't realize she had something planned every day with her crew. I feel brushed aside. I've been gone, and I guess what they say is true: out of sight, out of mind. Lamya was putting her homegirls first, and they got her thinking that all I'm doing is talking behind her back.

I already found it strange that suddenly, our friend Rajkumari don't talk to me anymore and had unfriended me on social media. I suspect that Lamya had told her stuff that I said when I was planning my wedding. Rajkumari had been invited, but I took her off the guest list once she moved out of town, honestly not thinking she was even interested in coming, she had just moved, and for that simple fact, I thought it all worked out for the better.

*H*er baby's father *was* my brother Mack, who is my husband's good friend and a groomsman in the wedding. I had felt it was more than respectable to invite his current girl and first baby's mama, who is also a friend of mine. I did what I thought would be best, trying not to make people feeling uncomfortable.

I *had* told *all this to* Lamya *and told her not to* tell Rajkumari what I'*d* said. I didn't want to hurt her feelings. Basically, Lamya ignores me and starts telling everybody what I said, meanwhile telling me nothing. But God sees.

Our tension came to a head over Thanksgiving. She had invited me over for dinner, as usual. We had spent Thanksgiving together every year, minus the years I was gone.

she goes ahead and warns the *other* girls she *had* invite*d me*, letting them know everything we've talked about in our *prior conversation*. I *had asked her not to bring it up. I* sense*d* she *was* blind to it all. We had *even exchanged* words. She *argues that* I've show*n* up at other events *with* this crowd, and I let her know that this issue was different. I feel she should protect me, as her best friend, instead of letting these people sit up and talk bad about me in front of her, and still not say a word in my defense. She claims she's done no such thing, but the proof is in the pudding,

Around November 28, 2019

I show up to Thanksgiving anyway, to show her how much I do care about our friendship.

I walk in, feeling good from leaving Auntie Kamal's house. I was full and warm off that Tequila. My attitude was happy, which is surprisingly because normally Tequila turns me into a beast.

I should have listened to my husband. He's been telling me to stay away and not go to Lamya's since she can't seem to respect my feelings as a best friend. But I didn't listen to him. I'm thinking, whatever, she's my friend, and ain't nobody coming in between us. Not you nor anybody else. Turns out, the joke's on me.

When I entered the room, I *immediately* felt the energy was bad. I said "happy Thanksgiving" to Kira. *She* says nothing back. *A mutual friend of ours say she does respond, but* I didn't know who's side she was on. This is the same girl who just said all my bridesmaids were ugly, we were divided. We weren't partying together. Kira is obviously pumped up already. I wasn't feeling her and she wasn't feeling me. Lamya wants us all together so badly, she doesn't care who's uncomfortable at this point.

Later in the night, Maeva and I are in the garage. She's smoking a cigarette, we're talking, and she mentions to me how she had to tell Lamya that I would often call to check on her and let her know I love her. Then, unexpectedly, she asks me if I had called Lamya a fat ass.

Around November 28, 2019

I'm thinking in my head, *what are you talking about? First of all, how* petty *do* you guys *have to be to* take my kindness for a weakness? *Secondly,* I *honestly* don't know *when I have ever called Lamya any names like that. All I can think is, sometimes* that's how I describe people when I'm faded, playing, *just joking around.* Heck, I even call my husband "ugly" and "stinky ass" sometimes. I'm just playing out of love, and I never mean to hurt anyone's feelings.

I thought for a bit and figured out that the rumor may have started when I was in Arizona for my training to be a driver, *and I* had call Lamya *to* ask her *if she thought our friend* Melissa, *who* lived *in* Phoenix, had shiny black shoes I *could* borrow for my uniform inspection that Wednesday. I had brought the wrong color shoes.

Melissa ends up coming to my hotel room, we have a drink, we're talking, laughing, enjoying each other's time. We talk about Lamya and a few other things, and I must have laughingly said "I love Lamya's fat ass" or responded to something jokingly that way. On God, I swear I never meant anything wrong out of that.

Over the course of the night, Kira and her friend leave at one point to go to the store. Once they're gone, Lamya brings to my attention that Kira had said she doesn't know why we aren't cool. Are you kidding me? It seems like if everybody has so much to say when I'm not around, and I'm sick of it. I'm here now, so let us get everything out on the table like real women.

Once they come back. Lamya is trying her hardest to get everyone together. We're dancing, taking shots, she's recording us on Snapchat, trying to have a fun time. The energy is fake. I can't take it. I haven't been talking about Lamya like everybody seems to think, so tell me, what did I say? And if the only thing y'all can come up with is that I called her a fat ass... really, you kids? I really want to know what is up.

Suddenly, I say something to trigger Lamya. She hops in my face mad, not wanting me to say what I had to say. Everyone is twiddling their fingers now. No one says a thing, and I think it's pathetic. "Right. My point exactly! You are all messy and talk about each other. I'm too old for this."

Healed

I turn to Kira then and ask, "Are we cool now or what?" I've been giving you a pass cause you Reg sister and I've been letting you get away with slick stuff I want to know if I must worry about her and her bad vibes after this. I didn't like her energy towards me at all. I know she talks crap, and I'm tired of it. I figured, if we were going to continue being around, we might as well say how we really feel.

The last time we had been in each other's presen*ce was* at *Aaliyah's birthday* dinner. *The* energy between us was all bad then too. I was there talking with another friend Monica, and suddenly Kira intruded in on our conversation. She wasn't even being addressed, and there she was being rude about me and my man. Maeva happens to be on the phone with her husband nearby, and she thought it was so funny she had to tell him what was going on.

I gave Kira a pass that night, but I wasn't happy about it. Last I checked, you didn't want him and I'm not your homegirl. I don't owe you any loyalty.

After that, I would still see her around, but it wasn't like I had to be around her all the time. We would keep our distance.

Flash forward again to Thanksgiving at Lamya's house, I let her know I had chosen not saying anything to her that time because she's Reg's sister, and I had lots of love for Reg. "But it's time you mind your own business and stop with the slick talk. I'll be the one to tell you, since Lamya ain't saying it."

From there, she started talking loudly, taking off her lace frontal and earrings, getting ready to fight. What I should have done was take off on her right there, but I didn't want to fight. That wasn't my intentions. She is telling me how skinny I am, all this and that. I'm thinking, who cares? I never had a problem getting a man and keeping him. I just wanted her to shut up and leave me alone.

*Then s*he gets in my face *and* puts her hand around my neck. *Mind you,* she's bigger than me. *Still, I'm not wanting to fight.* I politely take her hand off my neck. God was really working on me. The old Lacole would never have let any of that go down.

After I get her hands off my neck, she hits me in the eye.

At that point, I must defend myself. I lose it from there. All I could think of was, God, please forgive me and give me the strength. He was on my side. He did not want to see me go back to jail.

She should have made that first hit the last hit. All I can say is, they better be glad Maeva's husband was there. *He pulls me back,* pushes me on the floor and threaten to handcuff me. When he threatens to cuff me, I thought to myself, why was I the one he chose to attack?

I was the smallest in the house, and I got hit first. I thought we were cool, Mr. Officer. I have given you rides to the store before and everything.

Come to think of it, I can't be mad at him though. It's not his fault that all he hears is negativity about me. He's just attacking who they were all attacking. It all made sense once I had collected my thoughts and gotten out of there.

*In the end, i*t worked out for the better. I knew my capability once she hit me and it didn't hurt. I knew I had the upper hand, and Lamya did too. That is why they were protecting her.

They were saying, my godson Butter is in the room now to see this. I laughed. It's ok to bomb on me in the house, so long as my godson didn't, see?

I was telling her to come outside, but she refuses. I sensed that at that point, she felt she had one up on me, and she wanted to keep it that way. I gave her that. I guarantee that if it had been the other way around, they all would have come outside. They love seeing people fight at Lamya's house.

So, I leave. I'm hurt. I didn't know which way to turn. I didn't want to tell anybody about this, so they can all slap me in the face with "I told you so." I did not want to hear that at all.

I felt so humiliated and embarrassed that I got kicked out of my best friend's house for trying to defend myself, and they're all saying it's my fault because I said what I said. Who cares what I said? Nobody shouldn't put their hands on me, period. Especially in a friend's home, where I feel safe. It's not like I was disrespecting Lamya house or Kira's brother. If anything, she disrespected the house.

They're all saying it was my fault what happened, that I came to Lamya's house pumped up, wanting to fight. All of it is lies. How is that possible? There's no way I came in ready to fight and I still let her do all what she did to me. Lamya knows I'm the type of person that stays ready. I didn't fear anything or no one.

After what happened on Thanksgiving, everyone who was in the house, who were supposed to be my friends, all reach out to my sister Lakeyna, talking mess about who said what. Lamya and Maeva starts trying to turn Lakeyna against me, telling her that I didn't want her in my wedding, trying to hurt her.

I couldn't believe what they were telling Lakeyna. She's my sister, my only sister that was here to support me. Even if she wasn't supporting me like I felt she should have, she was still going to be in my wedding.

I didn't understand it. Lamya's mad and hates me that much. She's trying to turn everyone against me, trying to continue hurting me. And that made me mad. I was going through different feelings and emotions at that point, lashing out at people, but not purposefully. I wanted to take Lamya's head off. It got bad. I never felt that way about her.

At the end of the day, everything that happened just showed me Lamya's loyalty. She had betrayed me, and that's all I needed to see. Now our friendship made sense to me. But I don't think Lamya understands the severity of it. She told others that what she did and how I felt wasn't that serious.

I do not know if Lamya looked at me more as a competition or what. She *often* spends time together with girls younger than her. I was trying to piece it all together. There was never any competition in my eyes. She always had it made; her dad handed everything to her. I admired that. I loved everything about it.

Everything was always a struggle for me. If anything, I wished I could have been like her. I never once thought I was better.

I hate to say it, but now that I'm grown, I look back and know that friends don't do friends like we did each other. Our relationship was always toxic, I just couldn't see it. I was too young and dumb. I thought it was normal.

Once I realized that, I knew that our relationship was never going to go anywhere. We had grown apart, and in my opinion, we were on vastly different maturity levels. It was time for me to move on, as badly as it hurts. We didn't see things the same, and I wouldn't try to force it any longer. I gave up. I'm done. You can have her. I'm done with anything or anyone that requires fakeness.

The only thing that hurts about this situation was that I loved my godson Butter. I had just come back into his life after being in prison. I was sad, thinking to myself that I won't be seeing him anymore unless he reaches out to me when he's older. And even then, they have him thinking it was all my fault.

I will always love Lamya for what she's done for me. But I'll never be able to live past the betrayal I felt. That's something I never want to feel again. If anyone owed me loyalty, it was her, my best friend.

Me having her back the way I did, coming home, saying I wanted to be the best friend *she* never had, *all of that meant something to me. But in the end, I can say it* all worked out for the better. I will not continue getting sucked up in the Southeast web, letting individuals get away with mistreating me.

I'm a good person, and I would say it's a privilege to be around me. When I did wrong, I had to suffer the consequences. I'm somebody, whether others want to believe it or not. I stand firm today, on God's word. If I respect you, you will respect me; if not, that's ok too, you won't be around me.

If you have a good friend today, appreciate that person. Make sure you both are on the same page with each other's hearts. Love that person. From time to time, make sure they know they are special to you. They don't make good people the same, and a good friend is hard to come by.

Not too long after that, I started to realize that I had been falling back from God, with all these different distractions I had going on in my life. That's why all this was happening.

God knows when your priorities stray! I needed to get back on track and realize who comes first in my life. I needed to stop with all this madness.

I joined the Church of the Living God, which is my husband's family church. That church made me feel like part of an even bigger family.

I got baptized in February by the same pastor Jones who had married me and my husband. I felt honored. Tooper even started going to church with me.

I start driving for UPS right around peak season. My first day was October 1, 2019. Work was slow for me because I was a new driver. It was a lot of responsibility, and there was a lot you had to learn fast.

Money was great every week. I couldn't believe God has blessed me with this good paying job with benefits. I really felt normal.

As soon as work started to slow down, I had time to just be happy. I was tired. I was working six days a week, doing overtime, and I was frustrated because I had gotten in my first small accident.

I hit a rain gutter over a garage driving a U-Haul, something I wasn't trained to drive. It was much bigger than the UPS package car. I had to maneuver my way out of the situation, and it obviously didn't work. Being a driver came with more challenges than I thought.

March 2020 hits, and I'm blessed to still have a job despite the Coronavirus shutting down must of the economy. Work picks up massively, and it's a little scary that everybody is off but us. We drivers are considered essential workers. People in the warehouse are getting the virus.

I make sure to always keep my mask tight and social distance. I'm not trying to bring the virus home, but I ain't complaining — the money is excellent, and I'm working a good amount of overtime and it feels good to deliver packages to make others happy in this situation.

Tooper and I are making sure we're taking all the precautions we see on the news when we get home from work, to try and stay safe as possible. We're trusting God and the process.

Everything is good we are out my sister's house but. We still need somewhere permanent and comfortable to live. I don't want to move just anywhere. I pray on the situation and tell God what I'm looking for. On God's timing, I'll get it.

A few months later, God blesses me with exactly what I'm looking for. Something nice, no more than two neighbors, in a nice location. If it is not God watching over me, then what is it? I don't believe in simple luck when it comes to me.

I am loving my new place and how I've hooked it up. It's perfect for me and Tooper. He is doing good, getting closer to God, staying clean, working, going to school. He's getting closer to being done and he's staying focused on the finish line. We bought a 26-foot box truck to start our own business, Tole Transport, so we can have a third income on the side.

Psalm 27:1 *The Lord is my light and my salvation; whom shall, I fear? The Lord is the stronghold of my life; of whom shall I be afraid?*

2 When evil men advance against me to devour my flesh, when my enemies and my foes attack me, they will stumble and fall.

3 Though an army besiege me, my heart will not fear; though war break out against me, even then will I be confident.

4 One thing have I asked of the Lord, this is what I seek: that I may dwell in the house of the Lord all the days of my life, to gaze upon the beauty of the Lord and to seek him in his temple.

5 For in the days of trouble he will keep me safe in his dwelling; he will hide me in the shelter of his tabernacle and set me high upon a rock.

6nThen my head will be exalted above the enemies who surround me; at his tabernacle will I sacrifice with shouts of joy; I will sing and make music to the Lord.

My goal is to continue putting God first, being the best wife I can be, staying successful as an entrepreneur, and keeping my circle tight. My trust level is extremely limited these days. I feel God didn't place me on this earth today to have many friends. Instead, I believe that what was revealed to me was for a purpose: to use this time to share what God had done for me and what he can do for you. When I consider my past and my life, I would say I'm a miracle. I will never be perfect, but I continue to strive for something higher.

You can overcome anything you put your mind to. You can be the smartest person on earth, but if you don't apply it, it means nothing. If you don't use it, you will lose it. Tap into your creative side. A mind is a terrible thing to waste.

Don't waste your life going out like I did in my youth. Know that there are ways to break the generational curses Don't let your past hinder you or be the reason you don't achieve. If you think that way, you are not allowing yourself to grow into the sunflower God created.

Trust God. He will give you the desires of your heart. Keep God first.

This is my living testimony. Life is too short to walk around unsure about what you're doing. Have faith, even if it starts out as small as a mustard seed. Nurture that faith, until it grows to be bigger than your fears. Work on yourself and vibe alone for a while. Be still and know that He is God.

I'm a living witness that God will change your life if you allow Him to. Surrender.

Matthew 6:19-21 *Do not lay for yourselves treasures on earth, where moth and rust destroy and where thieves break in and steal, but lay up for yourselves treasures in heaven, where neither moth nor rust destroys and where thieves do not break in and steal. For where your treasure is, there your heart will be also.*

Matthew 6:33 *Do not seek material things. But seek first the kingdom of God and his righteousness, and all these things will be added to you.*

None of us is perfect; He wants us like that. He knows were filthy rags that fall short of His glory every day, and he still loves us.

I don't question God's work. I have such absolute confidence in God's plan, I don't even get upset anymore when things don't go my way. I continue to pray and be patient.

Pick up a Bible read.

Psalm Proverbs chapter 3:5 *Trust in the Lord with all your heart, lean not on your own understanding in all your ways acknowledge him and he shall direct* your path. Matthew 7:7 *Ask, seek, knock and it will be given to you.* Matthew 6:25 *Therefore I tell you don't worry about your life.*

> Pastor Randell G. Knighton, of the Church of the Spirit of God:
> *Praising his name (Proclaiming)*
> *Request his mercy and answer (Petitioning)*
> *Engaging his heart (Pleasing)*
> *Seeking his face (Devote)*
> *Staying in faith (Perseverance)*

Don't be like I was in my earlier days before I went to prison. I was lukewarm about going into the church house and came out the same way I went in, with really no intentions of changing for the better.

Actions speaks louder than words. I knew what was right, I just wasn't doing it for whatever reason. I would go in the church house, praise God, then walk out and go straight to hang out at bars, partying with married man, stealing, lying, robbing, doing everything under the sun that wasn't right.

Everyone makes mistakes in life. That doesn't mean they have to pay for them the rest of their days. Sometimes, good people make bad choices. It doesn't mean they are bad; it means there human.

Matthew 7:1-29 *Judge not that you be not judged. For with the judgment, you pronounce you will be judged, and with the measure you use it will be measured to you. Why do you see the speck that is in your brothers' eye, but do not notice the log that is in your own eye? Or how can you say to your brother, 'Let me take the speck out of your eye,' when there is the log in your own eye? You hypocrite, first take the log out of your own eye, and then you will see clearly to take the speck out of your brother's eye...*

1John 4:18 *There is no fear in love, but perfect love casts out fear. For fear has to do with punishments, and whoever fears has not been perfected in love.*

Psalm 100:3 *Know that the Lord, he is God! It is he who made us, and we are his; we are his people, and the sheep of his pasture.*

Matthew 6:24 *No one can serve two masters. Either you will hate the one and love the other, or you will be devoted to the one and despise the other. You cannot serve both God and money.*

Acts 20:29 *I know that after my departure fierce wolves will come in among you, not sparing the flock.*

Jeremiah 23:16 *Thus says the Lord of hosts: "Do not listen to the words of the prophets who prophesy to you, filling you with vain hopes. They speak visions of their own minds, not from the mouth of the Lord.*

1Corinthinians 2:14 *The natural person does not accept the things of the spirit of God, for they are folly to him, and he is not able to understand them because they are spiritually discerned.*

Luke 10:3 *Go your way; behold, I am sending you out as lambs in the midst of wolves.*

These are my favorite Bible verses from my time in prison.

Now turn on your stereo and listen to Marvin

Sapp, "The Best in Me" or Koryn Hawthorne, "Unstoppable" (feat. Lecrae). That will get you right.

Don't get sucked into thinking that what your parents did was right. Our parents didn't lead by example. It's true, what W.E.B. Du Bois said: "Children learn more from what you are than what you teach." We had no role models to look up to growing up. That's why I'm writing this book, to get a different message across. I can't possibly change everyone's life, but there must be one person who will read my story and decide to live differently. Just because our parents didn't have any interest in us, doesn't mean I don't.

My parents supported everything that I did that was wrong, from getting abortions to stealing and robbing. If they weren't supporting it, they were telling me how to do it.

They never took the time to try and sit down and talk to me with love and decency. They didn't think twice about my feelings or emotions as a young lady, how mentally traumatizing the things they did could be for me, how they could scar me.

Don't let it take going to prison for you to change your life. Reach out for help — it's okay to get help. Break those generational curses. Let's be better than what our parents taught us.

People tend to think you're crazy when you ask for help. It's not crazy to want to be better. What is crazy is not wanting to change.

Instruct your kids different. Give them a chance to see life from a unique perspective, a clearer point of view. Dream big and have goals. The world is a big adventure. Explore it and you will find that it's bigger than the same few friends and clubs. There's a world out there greater than Southeast.

I'm 37 years old. I would have loved to travel the world, to meet new people, learn different things and educate myself. Live your life to the fullest every day because we're not promised tomorrow. I've lost many people that I feel should still be here.

I never wanted kids. I was not ready. I knew what it took to raise them at an early age. If I had the option today, now that I'm married, I would have wanted to give birth to see what me and my husband could create. But God had a different plan, and I'm ok with that.

I cannot stress it enough to you. Do not take the route almost lost me everything.

You can't turn back the hands of time. What you can do is live in the time that is given you and make the best of it. Choose to do the right thing. Always have integrity. Treat others how you want to be treated. Get the hate out of your heart, whatever the reason for it. Know that that's not your battle; give it to God and let him take care of it. He will take care of it better than you can, I promise.

Let the haters hate. They will regardless, even when you're in your grave. There's no use caring what people think of you. Take care of yourself and put yourself first. Have boundaries, standards, morals. "You have limitless possibilities for your life," says Judge Lauren Lake. A person's character is shown in life.

Read Proverbs 26:11 *As a dog returns to its vomit, so fools repeat their folly.* You need only God!

Don't let men abuse you in any way or let them make you feel like you're not enough, like you're not the queen God created. Put limits and expectations on yourself. Know your worth. Often, strong women get misperceived as cold and mean, simply because they refused to be disrespected, mistreated, or taken for granted.

Get you a strong man who can handle a strong woman. A man who respects you for you and doesn't try and change you because they aren't able to handle you as you are, a strong woman. He shouldn't make you feel like there's something wrong with you for feeling like your everything. He should feel the same way. If he ain't willing to treat you right, there's someone else out there who is.

When the right man does put a ring on it, make sure he knows you appreciate him in every way, and you love him for being a good man. Turn on Beyoncé's "Dance for You" and set it off for him so he will know he's the most important thing in your life, and he won't even think about looking the other way. I'm speaking from experience, ladies.

You know the saying: One man's trash is another man's treasure. Don't settle for a man who's suffered from trauma his whole life and never wants to let it go and live past it to do better as a man. It ain't worth it. They call those men "boys," and all they are going to do is waste your time talking about the past. They will talk about what you need to change about yourself, because they don't want to face all the problems within themselves that are making them miserable inside, and so everything is your fault. There are too many fish in the sea for that, ladies.

Real women don't want boys. We want and need a strong man to protect and love us in every way, through the good and the bad. We want what my girl Monica calls Commitment:

Someone who knows how to listen and give me attention, who won't break my heart. I have good intentions. I ain't hard to please, I don't need a lot, just show me that you care. Can you be there when I need you the most?

I've been told, "Girl, you study, you work, you are responsible, you dress well, you put yourself together every morning, you manage your money, you are educated and respectful, you are loyal, and you have a vision and plans for the future. Who doesn't value that? Who doesn't deserve you?"

I wouldn't have wasted my time on none of that, if I had known all that I know today. It took me years to realize the need to research, read, and learn about what I was facing in order to survive and thrive.

Researcher shows that children of parents who have alcohol and drug issues develop their own psychology, dysfunction behaviors. Separation from the parents further exacerbates these psychological issues, leaving them in times to be very emotionally disturbed.

Some people, even when there young, can develop a personality that can be seen as cold or unfeeling, but on the inside is still a child with a need to be loved.

Those who have committed a crime, or is about to commit a crime, especially against someone that they don't know, they don't care about the consequences of their actions or what the consequences of their actions will be for others.

When a person comes from an abusive relationship and they meet another person who comes from a similar background, they end up perhaps becoming more attracted to one another because they can identify something they have in common.

Sometimes, when a girl grows up without her father, she's more vulnerable to needing a man whom she may view as being more of a fatherly figure, and that is usually someone who is much older.

When women feel the need to be wanted, it comes from the fear that they won't ever find someone to love them again. When people fall in love, it can feel like a drug rush, and not having that can feel like a withdraw.

For children growing up in a household where the parents aren't often there to take responsibility, having to take on adult responsibilities at such a young age really forces them to grow up much quicker than they should have to. In the process, they must deny a lot of their own needs they may have as children, in order to mature.

I knew none of this when I was growing up, going through it all. I had to teach myself how to cope when I realized I was suffering from all this.

So, make sure you do your research, if you do not know what's going on or if no one is willing to teach you. Teach yourself the right way to avoid destruction. You know the difference between good and bad. Value and love yourself enough to know you are worth working on.

I'm going to leave you with this verse:

2 Chronicles 7:14 NIV *If my people, who are called by name, will humble themselves and pray and seek my face, and turn from their wicked ways, then I will hear from heaven, and I will forgive their sin and will heal their land.*

THE END

Lacole Robinson from San Diego, California struggled her whole life until she found God then herself.